The Cat Who Cried for Help

Also by Nicholas H. Dodman

The Dog Who Loved Too Much

The Cat Who Cried for Help

Attitudes, Emotions, and the Psychology of Cats

Nicholas H. Dodman,
BVMS, MRCVS

BANTAM BOOKS

NEW YORK   TORONTO   LONDON   SYDNEY   AUCKLAND

Several different pharmacologic agents are mentioned in this book for therapy of behavior problems in cats. These drugs should only be prescribed by a licensed veterinarian who is familiar with their use. Drug doses vary considerably and side effects and idiosyncratic reactions may occur in some cases. In addition, many of the drugs referred to have not received formal (FDA) approval and a veterinary license. They may therefore only be prescribed when, in the veterinary clinician's opinion, they are truly indicated and when a veterinary label product that has the same action is not available. Also, the low protein diets referred to in the text should not be applied indiscriminately, especially in growing, pregnant, or nursing cats. Veterinary advice should be sought before instituting such a dietary change.

Bantam Books are published by Bantam Books, a division of Bantam Doubleday Dell Publishing Group, Inc. Its trademark, consisting of the words "Bantam Books" and the portrayal of a rooster, is Registered in U.S. Patent and Trademark Office and in other countries. Marca Registrada. Bantam Books, 1540 Broadway, New York, New York 10036.

PRINTED IN THE UNITED STATES OF AMERICA

To the memory of my sister,
Penny

Contents

Acknowledgments

I would like to thank Lynn Chu and Glen Hartley of Writers' Representatives, New York, for their support; my editor, Brian Tart, for his invaluable help with the manuscript; the faculty and staff of Tufts University School of Veterinary Medicine for their encouragement; the owners who graciously allowed me to tell their tales; and my family, Linda, Stevie, Vicky, Keisha, and Danny, for being there and making everything worthwhile.

Introduction

What would you do if your cat suddenly went psycho and started to attack you for no apparent reason, lying in wait and pouncing or stalking you with a faraway look reminiscent of its predatory cousins and ancestors? Or if two cats in your home, previously the best of friends, developed a mutual hatred so intense that every time they caught sight of each other they would end up rolling around on the floor, shrieking and spitting and creating enough havoc to raise the dead? Imagine the confusion of living with a cat that suddenly started biting its own tail until it bled or stripped off its fur until it was as bald as a coot . . . or of owning a cat who ate shower curtains, shoelaces, or running gear. What would you do and where would you turn for assistance?

Faced with such dilemmas, too many people take the easy way out (for them) and take the cat to a shelter or pound. Perhaps they salve their consciences by imagining that the cat has a fighting chance of being adopted, but they must know in their hearts that in all likelihood this is not the way it will turn out. Millions of cats meet an untimely end annually in the nation's shelters, pounds, and veterinary offices because owners erroneously believe their pets have unresolvable behavior problems. This is truly a sin of ignorance, one that sends a bad message to children about the disposability of life. Thankfully, there are many people who are devoted to the care of their pets and believe that a commitment of any kind should be honored. These people genuinely want to help their pets should they become ill or psychologically disturbed. I wrote this book for both groups of people, hoping to educate and inspire the former and to help the latter by providing real behavioral solutions.

The intention here is to describe, in narrative style through case studies, some common and some extraordinary behavioral predicaments with which cat owners may find themselves presented. The behavior that is causing the problem may be normal for the cat but inappropriate and out of context in the situation in which it occurs. Territorial aggression, urine marking, furniture scratching, and various nocturnal antics are all behaviors of this type. At the other end of the spectrum are behaviors that are truly abnormal, representing veterinary equivalents of human psychiatric conditions. Compulsive hair pulling, wool sucking, and feline hyperesthesia syndrome fall into this category. These conditions have concerned veterinarians for years, but the shift from believing that animals have no emotions or feelings to accepting that they have mental and emotional experiences similar to our own has opened up an entirely new way of understanding and curing behavioral problems.

The cases I discuss are ones I have treated at the behavior clinic of Tufts University School of Veterinary Medicine. The stories are true, though as they used to say on *Dragnet*, the names have been changed to protect the innocent. I attempt to paint an accurate picture of the consultation process, describing the human and animal suffering that these problems create, not for sensationalism but to illustrate the tremendous emotional investment some owners have in their cats and the dilemmas that confront the cats of the 1990s. The cases conclude with follow-up information describing the treatment that was pursued and how the case eventually was resolved. Each account should leave the reader better equipped to comprehend similar problems, or at least knowing what should be done and how to lobby for the correct treatment.

Many owners I see are at their wits' end and arrive at the clinic as a last resort, often against the advice of skeptics, hoping to find a solution for the problem. I know that if I am unsuccessful at turning the problem around, the owners have a limited number of options left. They have to either suffer with the problem, place the cat with someone else, or engage the ultimate solution of euthanasia. The tools of my trade are an accurate behavioral history, a precise diagnosis, and targeted treatment, which includes environmental adjustments, behavior modification therapy, and, if necessary, pharmacotherapy. Psychopharmacologic treatment features prominently in the treatment of behavior problems in cats, since cats are less amenable to retraining techniques than dogs.

There are three main classes of feline behavioral problems, and a section of the book will be devoted to each. The first section deals with various forms of *aggression*, including alpha cat syndrome, territorial aggression, fear aggression, redirected aggression, and pathological aggression. You will meet cats such as Ashley, who bosses his owner around and won't take no for an answer. Then there is Stormy, the Siamese who makes his owners' lives difficult by his relentless pursuit and bullying of their other cat, Penny. Sam, the cat of a student of mine, provides a focus for discussion of the true meaning of play and the fact that few (if any) kittens are actually psychotic. For an example of redirected aggression, it was hard to beat the story of Rubles the Abyssinian, who had a vivid encounter with a spinning dog only to take out his frustrations on his unsuspecting owner two hours later. Jonathan, the heiress's cat who turned out to have a medical reason for his sudden change of personality, provides a starting point for discussion of the many physical causes of aggression.

In the second section, on *emotional behavior*, fear, inappropriate elimination, excessive vocalization, furniture clawing, and sexual behavior are the subjects under discussion. My own two cats, Cinder and Monkey, feature in a discussion of fearful states that leads to the remarkable story of a human ailurophobe—someone with an irrational but pervasive fear of cats—and how she overcame her phobia. McTavish is the rebel without claws, and his case raises the thorny issue of declawing versus less-radical and more-humane ways of dealing with furniture scratching. Frankie, Gretchen, and Harry provide a potpourri of enlightening cases of inappropriate elimination behavior and provide guidance for owners of cats affected with this most common cat behavior problem. Next is the sad case of overattention to a "rescued" cat, Thomas, the cat who cried for help. His cries were not heard, however, and he ended up castrated, declawed, drugged, and devocalized. The discussion here centers on the question of whether cats should be confined in their own interest. As will be seen, the answer is not straightforward, and opinions run hot. The section ends with some interesting and confusing sexual problems that keep cat owners guessing. This chapter raises the issue of stray cats and the obligation of owners of nonbreeding cats to have their pets neutered.

Finally, there is a section on the fascinating but sometimes heartrending forms of *compulsive behavior*. Lucky, the wool-sucking cat, leads off the section, followed by a chapter describing the story of a calico cat suffering from the bizarre hair-pulling condition known as psychogenic alopecia. With psychogenic alopecia it's literally a case of hair today, gone tomorrow, and the poor calico was no exception. Then there is a tale about the curious and dramatic condition of feline hyperesthesia. This Tourette-like syndrome causes cats to exhibit peculiar grooming tics coupled with sudden mood swings and even hallucinations. The section concludes with a chapter on eating behavior in which over- and undereaters are put under the behavioral magnifying glass.

When questioned, a large percentage of cat owners claim that their cat has an unwanted "problem" behavior. Many of these owners are extremely dedicated people, but sometimes even they reach their limit. I am always surprised by just how much people will tolerate for their cats. I have seen homes sold and marriages dissolve as a result of conflicts over wayward cats, but despite the long fuses of dedicated owners, behavior problems are still a major cause of feline mortality. It is as important to understand your cat's behavior (and to know how to deal with problems when they arise) as it is to vaccinate it. This book is a tool to help people achieve the goal of better understanding, realize that something can be done, and know what that something is. Cats may walk by themselves, but there are times when they need our support.

Part One

Aggressive Behavior

One

Biting the Hand
That Feeds

Whatever you may have heard about the weather in New England, there are times when it is difficult to beat, especially in the spring and fall. Visions of spring haunt the natives all winter long, and when the season finally arrives, each day is cherished. One early spring day as I left for work, I realized it was one of those days. I stopped in the driveway and took a few deep breaths of the clean morning air. The sky was pale blue and cloudless except for a few thin streaks of cirrus. I stood there awhile just enjoying the scene. Eventually I headed for my car and started the short ride to Tufts University School of Veterinary Medicine to see a full list of patients. As I wound my way along Wesson Road (of Smith and Wesson fame) and turned down Willard Street (of Willard Clock Museum fame) I was trying to recollect the nature of my first case. The client had made the appointment late the previous afternoon as a "behavioral emergency." I wasn't quite clear what this meant, but I remembered being informed that the patient was a cat showing some kind of owner-directed aggression.

When I got to the hospital I ran upstairs, donned my white coat, and proceeded to the small-animal reception area, where I saw a case file marked for my attention. I scanned the front page, noting that the cat's name was Ashley and the owner was Mr. David Johnson. I turned around and looked for a likely candidate.

"Mr. Johnson?" I said, projecting my voice to the far side of the waiting room.

"That's me," said a tall, thin man with a goatee. He smiled faintly as he extended his hand in greeting.

He seemed a little tense, and I gathered he was nervous about the encounter. Glancing around for the cat carrier, I found that there wasn't one. I looked at Mr. Johnson quizzically. "Where's your cat?" I asked.

"Couldn't get him into the carrier, I'm afraid," Mr. Johnson admitted with a shrug. "Had terrible trouble. Eventually I decided that discretion was the better part of valor and left him at home."

I glanced down and noticed that the insides of his forearms were badly scratched.

"Did your cat do that?" I said.

"Yes, he did," Mr. Johnson said, inspecting his forearms thoughtfully, "but not this morning. He did that a couple of days ago. I would have been nailed again today if I had persevered with him. Can we still go ahead with the appointment? I mean, can you still tell me what's going on without actually seeing him?"

"Well, it's not an ideal situation," I replied honestly, "but I can try to give you some idea about what's going on if you give me a detailed description of his behavior. I may even be able to reach a provisional diagnosis. It all depends on how straightforward the problem is. I will certainly have to see Ashley for myself at some point if I need to medicate him."

"Let's go ahead anyway," Mr. Johnson said emphatically. "I can always bring him in later if necessary."

We proceeded to the consulting room and took up our positions on either side of the desk. I instinctively liked Mr. Johnson. He seemed like a genuine, no-nonsense sort of person and was obviously very dedicated to helping his cat.

"Well, why don't you start by telling me what Ashley is like?" I prompted. Mr. Johnson cleared his throat and then began methodically to tell me all about his cat.

"He's an ordinary domestic cat, black and white, neutered, and about five years old. He weighed about eleven pounds at his last checkup."

"Where and when did you get him?" I questioned, probing the extremely important issue of Ashley's early experiences.

"From a friend when he was around six weeks old," Mr. Johnson replied. "He seemed happy enough where he was, with his mom and his littermates. I believe it was a good home."

"And when was he neutered?" I continued.

"Hmmm, that must have been when he was about six months old, I think. The usual age. I got him fixed to stop him from spraying . . . not that he had actually started spraying at that time, but I had noticed him beginning to react to cat fights outside the house and thought it would be just a matter of time."

"Did you notice any change in his behavior after he was neutered?" I continued.

"Not really," Mr. Johnson said thoughtfully, running his hand across his beard.

"I understand from the record that the main problem is one of aggression directed at you."

"Yes, it started about three years ago, when Ashley was two. Our local vet put him on Valium to calm him down a bit, and it seemed to work, so we kept him on it. Since then the aggression has been pretty much under control . . . until about two days ago, that is, when it suddenly flared up again."

"Tell me what happened."

"OK," he said, drawing himself up in his chair and once again glancing at the scars on his forearms. "The most recent incident occurred two days ago at around six o'clock in the evening. I had just finished petting him about five minutes earlier. He seemed in a pretty good mood. Anyway, I stopped petting him because I wanted to watch the news on TV, and that was when he attacked me. At the time I was sitting on the couch, not paying much attention to him, and he was next to me. Suddenly, for no apparent reason, he launched himself at me and bit and scratched my arm. I jumped up yelling and threw him off. There was another incident last night. He appeared to be fine right before the attack. My wife and stepdaughter had just finished petting him, and he was lying peacefully on the carpet in the living room. I walked by a short while later, and he jumped up and attacked me. I noticed that his tail was big and bushy. The hair on his back was standing up, and his ears were flat. Actually, now that I think about it, he made a howling noise right before he attacked. After that, I talked to him in soothing tones, and he seemed to calm down. Eventually he walked away, although he did come back a few minutes later, sniffing the air and appearing very tense. Then he wandered off again."

"That sniffing you describe could be what is called flehmen," I said. "Flehmen is a type of sniffing in which animals collect small quantities of odors into a specialized organ that acts as a nose within the nose, so to speak. Did he look up and gape as he did it?"

"Yes, he did!" Mr. Johnson said, his eyes suddenly lighting up. "And as a matter of fact, he has done that flehmen, or whatever you call it, on other occasions before attacking."

"Maybe he's picking up a strange odor that triggers his sudden mood change," I suggested.

"But I don't think I was doing anything out of the ordinary," he said, looking puzzled "I hadn't been petting any other cats or anything, if that's what you mean."

The two of us thought hard for a moment but were unable to come up with any encounters Mr. Johnson had had that might have caused Ashley concern.

"Tell me about some of the other aggressive incidents," I said. "Maybe you'll remember something that will shed light on the problem."

"I don't know whether it makes sense to you, but in the past he has attacked me several times when I opened the refrigerator door. He came from nowhere and just launched himself at me. Who knows, maybe he was sitting on top of the refrigerator and I disturbed him when I opened the door. He's also attacked my wife and stepdaughter under similar circumstances. One other thing—if I disturb him when he's sleeping, he often jumps up, hisses and screams, and tries to bite me. And I've noticed he does a lot of twitching when he's sleeping, if that's any clue."

"I don't know about that," I replied. "Perhaps he's dreaming. Where does he sleep at night?"

"He sleeps on my bed and seems quite comfortable there. I've always thought he was quite attached to me. He brings me toys when he wants to play, and he's pretty persistent. He'll stand next to me making a half-meowing, half-purring noise and will meow louder and louder until he gets his way. If I don't get up when he wants me to, he bites my toes so that I have to get up."

"Does he bite people while he's on their lap and they're petting him?" I quizzed.

"Yes, he does, but he doesn't spend much time on people's laps. He's not really a lap cat. Most of the time when I pet him he's on the floor. He seems to like being petted, but sometimes I figure he's just had enough. He doesn't like me to fall asleep in my armchair. If I'm sleeping and he wants my attention, he'll come up and bite me in the hand until I wake up and pay attention to him. If I'm reading the paper, he'll come and sit right in the middle of it so that I can't see the page, or if I have it up in front of my face, he'll jump right onto it and collapse it on me. After he gets fed in the evening, if he's still hungry, he'll come and nip at my ankles or toes until I give him more food. He certainly has his own way of communicating. He has quite an imagination, too. He has a stuffed squirrel that he chases, and when he gets it he drops it in his food dish and then proceeds to eat all around it."

"That sounds like predatory behavior," I told him. "Is there anything else I should know about him? Tell me more about the attacks that occurred before he was medicated."

"There were about five or six attacks before we went to the vet's," he said. "I remember that some of them occurred immediately after we were petting him. Some of the other assaults were those refrigerator ambushes I told you about earlier. Something else you might find interesting is that he was one of a litter of five, and the four other people who owned his siblings have had to get rid of their kittens because they were hyperactive and aggressive. I know that because I've stayed in touch with the breeder. Maybe this thing runs in families, whatever it is."

"Hmmm, that's interesting," I mused, thinking it did sound very much as if it was genetic. "Tell me one more thing before we move on to filling in my aggression score sheet. How does he react to strangers, and how is he in your veterinarian's office?"

"Oh, he likes strangers. He bullies them a bit, the way he bullies me. He comes up and nips them to get them to play with him, and he's satisfied only when he has their undivided attention. He's a curious cat. He explores the people and whatever they have with them and is noted for jumping into people's pocketbooks. At the vet's it's a totally different matter. He turns into a raging, seething mass of fur, claws, and teeth. The vet has actually said, 'This cat is totally insane.' "

I was beginning to get a picture of a fairly confident and determined cat who liked to get his own way, although some of the aggressive responses did seem a little odd in the sense that they were out of proportion to the trivial nature of the provocation. I was also concerned about the flehmen reaction that preceded some of the more savage attacks.

As I pondered the situation I handed Mr. Johnson a questionnaire that I normally use to evaluate dominance aggression in dogs. At the time I had only just begun to confirm my suspicion that cats, too, display dominance aggression toward people, and I had not yet developed a feline-specific questionnaire. I watched with interest as Mr. Johnson checked off boxes indicating that Ashley had had aggressive responses to thirteen of thirty challenges. These challenges included walking past the animal while it is eating, taking away a stolen object, disturbing it while it is sleeping or resting, lifting it up, petting it, handling its feet, reprimanding it in a loud voice, walking by it when it is on a bed or furniture, and trying to make it respond to a command. Ashley's response was to growl, hiss, or bite in these situations. Because his response profile corresponded so closely to that of a dominant dog, I diagnosed feline dominance-related aggression as at least part of his problem, but I had a feeling that something else was going on, too.

Despite popular opinion to the contrary, cats can form despotic social hierarchies under certain circumstances. In such an arrangement there is one leader, the alpha cat, with other group members sharing second-in-command status. Occasionally a third

social class, the pariah, is evident. The latter individuals are basically outcasts who get pushed around by everyone else. It appeared that Ashley regarded himself as the leader of the Johnson
family and perceived other family members as subordinates. I
hoped they hadn't sunk as low as pariah status. If Ashley was the
alpha individual in the house, he would likely use escalating aggression to get (or keep) whatever he wanted, with very little
respect for the needs of others. This description fit the facts well.
I explained my ideas to Mr. Johnson and proceeded to advise him
on how to deal with Ashley.

"I tell you what I would do," I began. "First, avoid any confrontations between Ashley and yourself. I would like you to ration his petting attention for a few weeks, and please advise your
wife and stepdaughter to do the same. In addition, I would like
you to find some way of keeping him off the refrigerator. You
could block his access to it, or you could booby-trap it with
upside-down mousetraps, which work like harmless land mines.
Also, look around before you open the refrigerator door and make
sure he's not lying in wait. With regard to his mealtimes and nap
times, I want you to avoid approaching him while he's eating, and
don't wake him up while he's sleeping. Never reprimand him,
and don't try to make him do anything he doesn't want to do.
Above all, don't pick him up even if he yells for attention. All his
toys should be put away, and you should let him have them or
play games with him only on *your* terms."

"How exactly do I do that?" Mr. Johnson asked.

"You should keep all his stuffed toys in a drawer. When the
mood takes you, go to the drawer, call him to you, and *if* he
comes, give him the toy and play with him. If the game looks as if
it's getting out of hand and he gets belligerent or demanding,
give a cease command and leave the room. Instead of the word
cease you could use a benign stimulus, such as a duck call, to

signify the end of the game and signal that you are about to deprive him of your attention."

"I see," Mr. Johnson reflected, looking interested.

"Moving on to food and feeding," I continued, "you should let him know that you are in charge of the food department and that he needs to do what he's told if he wants to be fed. Feed him twice a day, but *only* if he responds to a signal. Call his name or tap on a food can. If he comes, give him his food and leave him in peace to eat it. Give him enough so that he won't be hungry when it's finished, and don't hang around to make sure he has had enough. Pick up any food he leaves and put it away until the next mealtime. He will soon become more respectful to you and your family. Set limits for him and stick to your guns. Instead of being his waiter, you will become his leader and provider—a whole different spin."

"This all sounds so logical. I don't know why I didn't think of it myself," Mr. Johnson said, and smiled.

"In the future," I exhorted, "you should give him what he wants only if he does something to deserve it, and that includes your attention. Please try keeping him off your bed and the couch because these have been problem areas in the past. His authority is increased by giving him access to these elevated locations, from which he launches some of his scarier attacks. In these situations, he is, in a manner of speaking, king of the hill. One easy way to keep him off your bed is to shut the bedroom door so that he can't get in. The same strategy may work for the couch during the day, depending upon how practical that would be in your home. Alternatively, you could try remote punishment, like the upside-down mousetraps we discussed earlier. That will make these places less desirable. If you don't like the idea of mouse-traps, there are little plastic springers you can buy in a pet store that do the same thing."

"Mousetraps sound fine to me," Mr. Johnson interjected.

"Finally, you should be teaching him a trick every month. It doesn't have to be anything fancy, just something that he does on cue for you. Using a clicker can be very helpful. A clicker delivers a single distinct click that is paired with a reward, usually a food treat. Ashley will quickly learn to associate the click with the treat, and eventually the clicker alone will signify that he has done something right. Initially you should reward him with a click and a treat for doing something close to what you want him to do—say, taking a few steps toward you when you call his name. Once he has achieved this level of response, delay rewarding him until he comes closer than the time before, and so on. This technique is called shaping, and it involves training by successive approximations to what you eventually want him to do. Training with a clicker is faster and more effective than using verbal acknowledgments or food treats alone."

Mr. Johnson nodded his understanding.

Before Mr. Johnson left I discussed one more thing with him: medication. Since I could not prescribe medicine directly for Ashley, I had to enlist the cooperation of his local veterinarian in this venture. I informed Mr. Johnson that I would write a letter to his veterinarian offering some suggestions about Ashley's medical management. My plan was to wean Ashley off Valium because it wasn't working and also because it has been shown to cause liver problems in some cats. I suggested phasing in a Prozac-like drug called Anafranil. The goal of the pharmacologic treatment was to spare Mr. Johnson subsequent attacks during a retraining program. He asked for some clarification regarding my recommendation of Anafranil. I thought he might find the rationale difficult to understand but tried to explain as best I could using layman's terms.

"Anafranil, like Prozac, increases the availability of a brain chemical called serotonin. Serotonin has mood-stabilizing *and* antiaggressive properties. Low levels of serotonin are associated with aggression and impulsivity. As serotonin increases, aggression decreases, but paradoxically dominance is enhanced at the same time. Since I've told you that Ashley's aggression is related to dominance, you might think it sounds odd that aggression and dominance are inversely related, but it's not so odd when you consider how dominance is maintained. Dominance is a dynamic state that is achieved as a result of social interactions. By engaging in and winning aggressive encounters, dominant animals drive up serotonin levels and gain in composure. As the serotonin levels fall, the aggression threshold is lowered once more, making attacks more likely. It's almost as if dominant animals are serotonin junkies and need to engage in an aggressive encounter to get a fix. Anafranil may stabilize dominance aggression by keeping serotonin levels high, thus reducing the necessity for frequent aggressive encounters. I have had several aggressive cats become quite placid within a few days of starting Anafranil or Prozac."

"Well, I feel we should try the medication," Mr. Johnson said as he packed up to leave. "I just don't feel safe in my house anymore."

"Please call me weekly to let me know how things are going," I urged. "You should make a note of any further aggressive incidents so that we have an accurate record of what's going on. Call me anytime if you have a question or if there's a problem. Remember, I would still like to meet Ashley, so if you can get him into a carrier sometime, give me a call and come on down. Let's schedule a follow-up appointment for three or four weeks from now anyway and trust that you will be able to apprehend him at that time."

"It sounds like a plan," Mr. Johnson said, and we bid each other farewell. He left clutching the various handouts I had given him.

So what was really going on with Ashley? Was he just a dominant cat, or was his behavior really out there in left field? The answer was a bit of both. Many behaviorists would have diagnosed Ashley's condition as petting-induced aggression because he displayed aggression while he was being petted or shortly afterward. Cats that show this type of aggressive behavior may initiate an interaction with a person by jumping up on his or her lap. The unwitting person acquiesces to what appears to be a benevolent request for petting, but moments later the metamorphosis begins. The transition is heralded by the cat delivering meaningful glances at the owner's hand while impatiently twitching the tip of its tail. If these telltale signs are ignored, the real trouble begins, and biting and clawing of the hand that feeds is the all-too-common outcome. The premonitory gestures of sideways glancing and tail twitching should be interpreted as evidence of impending hostilities, but that isn't always the message that well-meaning cat owners glean from their cat's behavior. Misunderstanding the events, they continue to pet their cats more earnestly, hoping to achieve a degree of reconciliation. Some owners misconstrue the behavior as "love bites" and persevere in spite of continued biting. Victims can be identified by the scars on their hands and forearms. Ignoring the early signs of this (literally) repulsive behavior can have serious consequences, as the attacks may escalate into more-purposeful bites. By the time this stage is reached the cat is highly aroused, and even if the owner attempts to withdraw, the incensed cat may pursue him or her with resolve. Cats that engage in such domineering behavior are not shy. Quite the reverse—they are usually confident and independent. Indeed, they are quite dominant.

I became aware that cats with petting-induced aggression show other signs of pushy aggressiveness soon after I saw my first few cases of this condition. One woman reported that her cat would not let her sleep in the morning and would jump on the bed and bite her on the nose until she got up. Another reported that her cat would jump at the newspaper while she was reading it, knocking it out of her hands. Still others reported having their cat nibble at their ankles while they were preparing food for it (presumably because they weren't opening the can fast enough) or biting their hand if they fell asleep in an armchair. It became clear to me that petting-induced aggression wasn't a specialized form of feline aggression, but rather a component of the larger syndrome of dominance. The parallels with canine dominance were uncanny. Some dominant dogs also become aggressive when you start or stop petting them—it's one of the hallmarks of the condition. How they react depends on the mood they're in at the time. Like dominant cats, dominant dogs are bossy and self-sufficient. In addition, their owners also tend to be on the compliant side, setting up a similar human-animal relationship. I was sure I was on to something.

Since hierarchically dominant cats are rarer birds than their canine counterparts, one might expect owner-directed dominance aggression in cats to be less prevalent than it is in dogs. This does indeed appear to be the case. I am convinced that the syndrome occurs, and because of my conviction I have stopped using the term *petting-induced aggression* in favor of *feline dominance aggression* or *alpha cat syndrome* (borrowing from canine terminology). This approach has heuristic value and helps with the design of comprehensive management programs. It was these earlier revelations that cued me on how to interpret the aggressive behavior of cats such as Ashley and first caused me to start using my canine dominance profile questionnaire to evaluate them. I was sure that Ashley was a dominant cat, but I kept worrying about the significance of the recent escalation in intensity of the aggression and its relative unpredictability.

Owner factors may operate in permitting the expression of

petting-induced aggression. Owners of cats that indulge in this behavior have always struck me as warm, empathetic individuals who are kind almost to a fault. They often have considerable emotional investment in their pets and appear to treat them as equals or at least full-fledged family members. Such owners ask little in return for their affection and attention, but they do hope to be able to share a few pleasant moments with their pet from time to time. Is it too much to ask that the recipient of their attention might occasionally curl up in their lap without becoming aggressive? I don't think so, yet even this simple pleasure is denied to those who suffer the assaults of such cats. Textbooks sterilely proclaim that the treatment is to refrain from petting the cat. Doting owners are told to take heart from the fact that their cat will accept them in other ways. Such emollient statements are well-meant, but the advice is still a bitter pill to swallow. I have attempted a compromise, suggesting that owners should not refrain from petting their cats but should limit this attention and watch for early warning signs so that they can desist *before* the trouble escalates. This modified form of the advice permits owners some consolation and will reduce the number of aggressive incidents by avoiding confrontations.

The weeks slipped by after my appointment with Mr. Johnson, and still I had heard nothing from him. I was beginning to worry that things weren't going well. Despite my concerns, he did eventually contact me and informed me that he wanted to bring Ashley in at the earliest opportunity. I didn't know why he was suddenly so optimistic about his ability to get Ashley into the carrier but was delighted to hear from him and scheduled an appointment for the same day.

I had several other cases to see before Ashley and had to pick up the pace to ensure that I would be free at two o'clock, the time scheduled for Ashley's visit. Two-fifteen came and there was still no sign of Mr. Johnson. I started to become concerned. Just then I had a phone call from him. He admitted that once again he had encountered some difficulty in getting his nibs into the carrier but had finally managed it. He wanted to know if it would still be OK for him to come in for the appointment. Of course I said yes, and he left home right away.

Mr. Johnson arrived ten minutes later, smiling and reasonably unscathed, but judging from Ashley's compressed posture in the back of the carrier, I guessed the cat wasn't enamored by the prospect of a visit with the vet. I escorted Mr. Johnson to the behavior consulting room and started the interview by asking him to run through the events of the past few weeks. He related three episodes in which Ashley had become extremely disturbed. In one, some kids were playing noisily outside Mr. Johnson's apartment, running up and down the stairs and banging on the door as they flew past. This was too much for Ashley, who assumed full defensive mode, pupils dilated, tail bushy, and ears directed sideways. Mr. Johnson noticed that there was no hissing and that the incident was brief, lasting only a few seconds. A similar incident occurred after Mr. Johnson's young stepdaughter ran around the house making a commotion. A third incident occurred when Ashley heard a tracking device on the portable phone beep loudly. In this latter incident, Mr. Johnson reported that Ashley's pupils dilated "as wide as saucers" and that he emitted an ominous low growl. None of these events sounded much like the alpha cat syndrome. It sounded more like the something else that I had sensed initially—something along the lines of fear, perhaps, featuring a particular sensitivity to smells and noises. Unfortunately, behavioral diagnoses are often not exclusive, and Ashley's aggressiveness was shaping up as a composite problem. Perhaps Ashley felt the way he did because he was insecure and scared. But he may have reacted the way he did because dominance gave him the strength to deal with his problems proactively (to drive the boogeyman away).

I asked Mr. Johnson whether he thought the new medication and the dominance program were making a difference in Ashley's behavior, but as it turned out, he hadn't started either. Mr. Johnson's veterinarian had elected to increase the dose of Valium instead to see if that would help. I was disappointed about this news, so I contacted the vet directly and, with his approval, made the switch myself. Then I implored Mr. Johnson to try the program. After a couple of minutes of hearing about his busy schedule, I finally managed to persuade him to put in the time.

Then came my attempt to give Ashley a physical examination and take a blood sample. Mr. Johnson slowly opened the door of Ashley's carrier, and we both stared into its dark interior for a while, waiting for him to grace us with his presence. There was nothing doing. Changing strategy, Mr. Johnson got down on his knees and tried to pull the little warrior out of the carrier by his front feet amidst much hissing and spitting. Ashley was not amused by these attempts and held his ground. His head was held low and his elbows jutted out sideways as he hunkered down more resolutely in a ready-to-strike position.

"Boy, he looks scared," I said to Mr. Johnson, not feeling all that brave myself.

Perhaps one of our expert animal technicians would have some luck in coaxing him from the box to get a blood sample, I thought. I made a quick call to the front desk, and one of the nurses came immediately to the consulting room. I told her about Ashley's mean streak, advising strict caution, and she whisked the carrier away to the wards. Mr. Johnson and I had been talking for only a few minutes after the nurse's departure when she reappeared and summed up the situation in two words: "No way." Mr. Johnson and I looked at each other blankly as she elaborated on Ashley's fiendish behavior. Even with the benefit of towels, muzzles, and heavy gloves, none of our staff was prepared to risk life and limb to obtain a sample from Ashley while he was conscious. Round two to Ashley, but the match wasn't over.

The following week I called Mr. Johnson for a progress report. I was pleased to learn that he had begun phasing out the Valium and had been treating Ashley with Anafranil, as requested. He reported that Ashley was doing much better on the new treatment. There had been no further attacks, and Ashley was "not so annoying." Also, he had not been nipping at Mr. Johnson to get his way, and the noise sensitivity problem seemed to have been resolved. I was delighted with this report and encouraged Mr. Johnson to keep up the behavior modification so that Ashley's improvement would be maintained when he was weaned off the medication. Mr. Johnson and I agreed to talk again a couple of weeks later.

When I called Mr. Johnson two weeks later I found myself talking with a girl of perhaps five or six.

"Is Mr. Johnson there?" I asked hopefully.

"No, he's not here now," piped the child.

"Would you tell him I called, please?" I asked as politely as I could. "This is the vet. I'm Ashley's doctor."

There was silence for a moment, and then the girl spoke.

"Ashley's much better now. He's stopped growling and seems a lot happier. Actually, he's much more lovable. You did want to know how he was doing, didn't you?"

"I sure did," I said, smiling to myself, "and you've said a mouthful. Thank you very much for the great report."

"You're welcome," she said. "Do you still want to speak to my dad?"

"I guess I should," I said, "just to check on a couple of things."

"OK, I'll have him call you. Bye."

I was stunned by the mite's grasp of the situation and thrilled to have what I knew to be an unbiased assessment of Ashley's progress. Mr. Johnson called me back when he heard that I had phoned. The word was good. Ashley was doing splendidly. There had been no further attacks, he had shown virtually none of the pushy behavior, and he seemed much more content. The only question that remained was when, if ever, could Ashley be taken off medication? As I was sailing in uncharted waters, I wasn't too sure of the correct answer to that question, but I informed Mr. Johnson that I didn't think that keeping Ashley on the medication would do him much harm if that was the way things worked out. The new medication was certainly less harmful than Valium. Of course, it would be preferable to wean him off Anafranil if possible, but we would wait and see. Whether we would wean him depended to some extent on Mr. Johnson's commitment to the behavior modification program. Mr. Johnson's decision was to keep Ashley on medication for the time being and to stay in touch. After all, he had had a nasty scare and Ashley had come awfully close to meeting his Maker. It is better to live with Anafranil than not to live at all.

Almost a year later Mr. Johnson returned to the clinic for a long-term follow-up visit. Ashley's improvement had been maintained, and yes, he was still on medication. There had been no alpha cat behavior and no sound- or smell-induced attacks. This time we got blood from Ashley, who was much more cooperative, and the results were a clean bill of health. I renewed the prescription because Mr. Johnson was still unsure about facing Ashley as he had been.

The only thing about Ashley's case that really puzzled me was the flehmen and the timing of some of the attacks. I still think that there was something else going on besides dominance. It may have been a mystery odor that aggravated Ashley. Odors are very important to cats because felines have a formidable olfactory apparatus. Cats sometimes attack their best buddies when they return from the vet's office, especially if they have stayed overnight or been subjected to anesthesia. Smell appears to be the motivation for such turncoat behavior. A dominant but suspicious cat such as Ashley would likely not take kindly to anything new or threatening in his environment. He certainly didn't care for the auditory invasions from within or without. Couple this with the fact that cats are champions at displacing their aggression onto some innocent target and you have another possible explanation for the weird attacks.

Less likely interpretations of his more animated attacks are that they were seizure-related or that they represented a form of feline schizophrenia. Perceptual alterations are known to occur in both conditions in people, and both may be associated with entirely inappropriate social behavior, including aggression. A strike against the schizophrenia theory is that the condition responded to the medicine the way it did, but in a cat experiencing olfactory hallucinations, who knows what brain chemistry would be involved? Ashley was dominant, of that I am sure, but I never did feel entirely comfortable with the ancillary diagnosis. Whether Ashley suffered from redirected fear aggression, a seizure-based problem, or a bizarre and as yet undocumented psychosis, I may never know. I do know that Ashley continues to do well on medication and that Mr. Johnson has no intention of weaning him off it at present. At least the conclusion of Ashley's case was satisfactory. Reportedly he is much more laid back these days, and his hair-trigger temper is gone. Indeed, there have been no aggressive incidents at all since he was medicated, and he seems to be enjoying life at last. From a feline assassin who would bite the hand that feeds him, Ashley has finally become a real pussycat.

Two

Give Peace a Chance

Now, it's one thing trying to patch up a squabble between cats, but it's another to try to cultivate a relationship between two cats that never did get along in the first place. We humans often assume that if we introduce two cats to each other they will enjoy each other's company and are bound to get along, as they have a lot in common—namely, being cats. Nothing could be further from the truth. Cats are as fussy as people when it comes to the company they keep and the space they are prepared to share. Most of us would not appreciate having a total stranger arrive unannounced in our home to share eating, sleeping, and bathroom facilities, and cats do not take kindly to this type of invasion (or even the threat of it), either. It is true that we, and our cats, may grow to appreciate the interloper, but escalating animosity is also a likelihood.

People, like cats, are most comfortable when they are familiar with their situation. Change is stressful. I once heard that three of the biggest stresses in life are bereavement, divorce, and relocation. It is intriguing that, even for humans, a geographic change, involving new acquaintances and new and unfamiliar territory, is one of the big stresses in life. Normally we go out of our way to keep things the same and to protect what is ours. We protect our families, our homes, and our land. It's the same for cats, except probably more so. Cats are extremely space- and distance-conscious. Up close, they have a zone referred to as their "personal space," where only bonded individuals are allowed. Friendly feline acquaintances are comfortable together within a "social distance," but not all socially compatible cats share personal space. A cat's territory is a much larger area that it will actively defend against infiltrators. Although territories may overlap, there is not always mutual tolerance. The happy coexistence of a number of socially acquainted cats within a household is a bit of a juggling act, achieved only through grace, good fortune, and an unlimited food supply. Unneutered males are particularly volatile, being somewhat preoccupied with supremacy and rank. Neutering is usually an effective solution for this particular problem. Most of the territorial problems I see originate in already neutered cats living together in what was a previously stable multiple-cat household. The problems are triggered when an unfamiliar cat is deposited in their midst or when one that has been absent for some time is returned to the throng.

Take the case of Stormy and company, for example. Stormy was a neutered Siamese cat that had cohabited blissfully for three of his six years with his Siamese pals, Rusty, MJ, and Penny, and his doting owners, Cynthia and John Piper. Then it happened. Cynthia received a phone call from a friend who owned Penny's littermate, Yoshiko. The friend announced that her husband had accepted a position in England and that they would be moving soon. The point of the conversation, however, was that she wanted Cynthia to adopt Yoshiko. The friend said she had agonized over the decision but in the end felt that it wouldn't be fair to Yoshiko to lug her all around the world in a cat carrier and then have her endure a mandatory six-month quarantine period.

What was one more cat, Cynthia thought, and a sib of Penny's to boot? It didn't seem like such a bad idea at the time, so she accepted. Yoshiko was dropped off early one morning a week or so later, complete with a six-month supply of food, a clean litter box, and some cat toys. Cynthia brought Yoshiko's carrier into her open-plan living area and opened the door. Yoshiko peeked out and began sniffing the floor in front of the carrier. Then she ventured out and started to explore more boldly. Stormy, Rusty, MJ, and Penny looked on from a distance. Nobody seemed particularly concerned by the new arrival. Stormy engaged in a little displacement grooming, and Rusty and MJ, after showing some initial curiosity, eventually sloped off. All was going well until Yoshiko came face-to-face with her sister, Penny. Apparently they didn't recognize each other, or if they did, the memories were not fond ones, because Penny suddenly lunged at Yoshiko, causing her to flee. Penny followed in hot pursuit, letting out loud screams along the way. Stormy had never seen anything quite like this before and sat there totally amazed by this turn of events. He wasn't so much agitated as profoundly interested. It was as if an entirely new dimension had been added to his life, which in fact it had.

By the time Cynthia had caught up with the feuding pair, Yoshiko had found a safe haven and Penny was strutting off victoriously. Territoriality was at the root of the dispute, and Yoshiko, the vanquished, had been relegated to lowly third-class accommodations. For a time at least, an uneasy peace reigned in the Pipers' household.

Lunchtime arrived without any further incidents, but Cynthia did notice Stormy and Yoshiko spending some time together, sitting close and apparently enjoying each other's company. Penny had been upstairs most of the morning but slid down the stairs just as Cynthia was about to bite into a sandwich. Cynthia stopped in midbite when she heard loud hissing. There was no mistaking this particular feline vernacular. There was definitely something seriously wrong. *Oh, no,* she thought, *Penny and Yoshiko are at it again.* But they weren't. It was Penny reacting vociferously because she was on the receiving end of some pretty nasty body language from Stormy. He wasn't actually chasing her at that point, but he was eyeing her in an extremely ominous way. Even Cynthia knew the meaning of the look she was witnessing, though she had never seen anything like it on Stormy's face before. Penny also was quite clear as to what the look meant and presumably had decided that noisy intimidation was a reasonable strategy—a good offense is the best defense and all that. The hissing and spitting continued. As Stormy scowled more intently, Penny escalated her noisy attempts at intimidation to an ear-splitting scream before she finally fled. And this was the way it was going to be for another year or so. Penny gave up chasing Yoshiko because she spent all her time looking out for herself, watching her own back. Stormy's evil eye was resolutely focused on Penny every time she went anywhere near Yoshiko, and every unpleasant encounter between the two invariably finished with Penny's expressing her displeasure vocally and retreating.

One year after this turbulent beginning, the fray escalated, and Stormy took a more proactive role in ridding himself of the menace. He would chase Penny mercilessly until she found refuge in the nether regions of the house. One of her favorite sanctuaries was on top of a tallboy in a spare bedroom upstairs. During one of Stormy's more aggressive pursuits of Penny, he endangered life and limb by chasing her on top of the stove and somehow turning on one of the burners. The Pipers were becoming extremely concerned about the way things were shaping up, but they didn't know where to turn. Things went from bad to worse. The following summer Stormy caught Penny for the first time and bit her severely in the rump. This conflict necessitated veterinary treatment: wound cleansing, topical treatments, antibiotics, the lot. Six months later there was another horror show when Stormy inflicted even more extensive damage, requiring surgical debridement of Penny's deep bite wounds under general anesthesia, the insertion of drainage tubes, and an overnight stay in a veterinary hospital. By this time the Pipers had had enough and kept the two cats separate most of the time, even though living that way in an open-plan house was tricky and inconvenient.

Eventually they talked with their vet, Dr. Gary Stuart, about the problem during a routine checkup. Dr. Stuart, one of our alumni, defied convention and recommended treatment with Valium. The Pipers were a little skeptical about the treatment but decided to give it a try because, as Bob Dylan said, when you got nothing you got nothing to lose. The Valium worked quite well for about eight days, but then Stormy started to have bouts of skin rippling and frenetic self-directed licking along his back. For some obscure reason it seemed that the treatment had triggered feline hyperesthesia syndrome, a seizure-based disorder. The vet advised the Pipers to discontinue the Valium and referred them to me.

I spoke with them on the phone first and, on hearing about the problem, suggested a house call. I chose to visit them partly because they lived right across the road from the veterinary school (so it was convenient) but also because I believed that it would be an advantage, in a case like this, to see the layout of the house. I hadn't made a veterinary house call for several years, so the experience was reminiscent for me of times gone by.

It was a cool early spring day as my car crunched up the Pipers' gravel drive. I set the parking brake and sat there for a few moments contemplating the scene. The house was of modern design, a cross between a Swiss chalet and an A-frame, and was situated in a pleasant neighborhood. The lawn and paths were immaculately kept, and there was an overall atmosphere of neatness and tranquility. I knew immediately that I would be dealing with conscientious, perhaps even fastidious individuals—always a plus.

I rang the doorbell and waited for what seemed like a long time before the door creaked open. Cynthia peered out from behind the door, smiled, and invited me to step inside. John Piper was sitting by a large coffee table in the center of their spacious living area. Light streamed through the windows, giving the whole scene a warm and friendly ambiance. At their invitation, I joined them around the table and made myself as comfortable as a visitor can be. I gazed around the house while Cynthia narrated the long but interesting story of Stormy and the gang. A wooden stairway wound up to a wide landing upstairs, and there were various doors leading off to the bedrooms. Because the home was open-plan, I could see every geographic point referred to by Cynthia during her narrative. There was the dining table, where it had all begun. There was the stove, where the conflagration nearly occurred, and there was the upstairs bedroom, which was a sanctuary for Penny. I was in heaven. Normally I have to conjure up these images in my mind.

As Cynthia's report drew to a close the cats began to grace us with their presence. First was Stormy, who appeared as a pair of deep blue eyes peering through the railings of the upstairs landing. Rusty was not far behind. The two of them melted down the stairs and joined us at a discreet distance, trying hard not to show that they were interested in the goings-on.

"Where do the cats sleep?" I asked.

"Stormy sleeps on our bed most nights," Cynthia replied. "I suppose that's because he's the boss. When he's not on our bed, he sleeps over there," she said, indicating a sofa in the living room.

"And where do the others sleep?" I probed.

"They sleep with him when he's on the sofa—except for Penny, of course, since she's banished. When he's on our bed, the others sleep on the sofa or on these seats we're sitting on. Don't worry, though," she said with a wry smile, "I vacuum the furniture every morning."

I didn't doubt it.

"Tell me," I asked, "does Stormy get along well with the other cats?"

"I think so," she replied. "He does have certain areas that he regards as his own, though. Sometimes he'll chase the others off or swat at them if they invade his space, but nothing comes of it, and the next thing you know, they're all curled up together again."

Yoshiko and MJ appeared momentarily but then sauntered off toward the kitchen to have another shot at willing open the food drawer. They were both smallish cats, aloof, graceful, and rather handsome with their seal points. It dawned on me that we had seen everybody except Penny.

"Where's her Ladyship?" I wondered.

"I put her upstairs in the spare room," John chipped in. "I suppose you'd like to see her, wouldn't you?"

"Very much," I replied, and he set off up the stairs to release her. Moments later he returned, and all eyes were directed upward at the now open bedroom door. For a while nothing happened, and we made small talk as we waited for the outcast to appear. Finally her slender form appeared, moving stealthily along the landing to the head of the stairs. She paused and then began an uncertain descent. At the foot of the stairs, the unwilling recluse paused and flashed looks in every direction. It may have been my imagination at work, but I thought I detected a slightly longer look reserved for Stormy. Penny slipped by and into the kitchen without much of a greeting for anyone. Poor Penny had become a pariah. Stormy never took his eyes off her, but he didn't make a move.

"Well, now that you've heard the sad story and met the gang, what next? How do we get out of this mess?" Cynthia asked.

"I'll be honest with you," I replied. "This is not the easiest of problems to solve. Some behaviorists go so far as to call it downright difficult bordering on impossible. Those folks usually recommend finding a new home for one of the feuding cats. Obviously the strategy works, but it's not an option most of my clients want to exercise."

"We would do anything rather than get rid of either Stormy or Penny," Cynthia said sincerely. "We would rather live as we do now, keeping them physically separated."

John nodded slowly, but he didn't seem quite as adamant as his wife on this point.

"OK," I said. "Here's what we'll do, but you're going to need to be patient because this can be a slow job. First I would like you to keep Stormy and Penny in different rooms with a closed door separating them. In the past you have always put Penny in the spare room and Stormy in your bedroom. With this arrangement there is no contact of any kind between them, and confining them to one exclusive area encourages the development of territories. What we must do is make sure that each is aware of the other's presence on the other side of a closed door, but we also confuse their tendency for territoriality by switching rooms. The switch should be made daily, taking great care not to let any escape-artist behavior confuse your plan. It's all too easy to let one cat or the other slip between your legs while you're changing the guard. Now comes the really tricky bit. You have to feed them simultaneously on either side of the closed door so that they can hear each other and catch scent of each other while they're eating. It's also good to pet them and play with them when they're like this so that they come to learn that wonderful things happen when they're together. The whole idea is to change their perception of what occurs when they're together. So far so good?"

"I understand what you're saying, but how do we phase in their reintroduction?" John asked.

"The first step, to crack the door an inch and secure it using a doorstop or hook and eye, is embarked upon only if there has been perfect peace on both sides of the closed door for at least two weeks."

"Understood," John acknowledged.

"Then be patient for a while until they're happy getting occasional glimpses of each other through the crack. If all is well, open the door four to six inches, but insert a narrow screen to prevent any physical contact. It's like a game of chutes and ladders. If things go well, you advance to the next level. If not, you have to go back to the stage before. Setbacks are inevitable and don't really matter as long as, in general, you're heading in the right direction. You just have to persevere until you succeed."

"The next step is to open the door?" John ventured.

"Correct, but you need a screen in place. I've seen my own cats desensitize to a neighborhood stray tomcat through a screen door without going through any of the previous steps, so this is a useful phase. But don't forget, give the cats time to get thoroughly used to each other before advancing."

"It sounds promising," said Cynthia. "I can't wait to get started."

"Well, there is one more phase I need to describe before you embark on the program," I interjected. "After all, you don't want them to have to live behind a screen. The next step is to reintroduce them to each other for a short while *in the same room*. At first they should be restrained with harnesses or in cat carriers, depending on how confident you are about the new peace, while they are allowed to eat. Each day, assuming things are still peaceful, bring them a little closer to each other and begin to extend the time they spend together. The primary goal is to have them eating side by side. Then one of them should be freed from the harness or carrier to see how things are really going. That will be bite-the-bullet time. It's a good idea to release the more passive cat first—in this case, Penny. If all goes well, you can try releasing Stormy next time, with Penny still restrained. Look for any signs of trouble. Finally it will be time for double, side-by-side freedom, and you just have to pray that they ignore each other and get on with their food."

"I see," Cynthia said. "So after that it's just a question of supervision for increasing periods of time before allowing them to be alone together."

"You've got it," I replied, "but remember—from the time they're allowed independence, you should continue to praise or pet them whenever you see them together. I expect that's a little different from what you've been doing."

"You've got that right," John said. "We mainly yell at them when they're behaving badly and ignore them when they're good."

"So does everyone else," I said.

The weeks went by and I had several conversations with the Pipers about how to fine-tune the plan. Things were going pretty well, but there had been a couple of setbacks and John was beginning to lose his initial enthusiasm for the program. Cynthia suddenly found herself single-handedly running the show. She had gotten to the point where she could leave the feuding pair alone for a short while and come back to find everyone still in one piece. The problem was that Stormy still occasionally flashed an evil eye or took a few steps toward Penny as if to intimidate her, and it seemed likely that the embers of discontent were still smoldering. Cynthia was pleased with the progress she had made, but she asked if anything else could be done to smooth the remaining rough corners. "Something like Valium," she suggested, "but not Valium."

It sounded like a riddle, but I had the answer: the anxiety-reducing drug buspirone (BuSpar). Buspirone is a designer drug virtually devoid of side effects, toxicity, and addictive potential, and it is an extremely effective treatment for anxiety. It also has antiaggressive properties. I thought that buspirone would be a reasonable and harmless substitute for Valium. Cynthia welcomed my suggestion, and Stormy's second round of medication was initiated.

Following a couple of dose adjustments, Stormy was finally in a much less hostile state. I presumed buspirone had something to do with this accelerated progress, although it's always hard to be sure. John was back to being supportive of the plan and was glad he had cooperated in giving Stormy a chance. Stormy wasn't a perfect angel from that day forth, but he was much more tolerant of Penny, and now neither cat has to be locked away when the Pipers go out for a few hours.

Not all cases of territorial aggression are as time-consuming to resolve as the Pipers', and not all require medication, though it does seem to expedite the reintroduction process. One time I amazed an owner and myself by resolving a yearlong intercat aggression problem in two days after taking great pains to explain how long and tedious the reintroduction process would be. This client opted for medication from the start, and once again buspirone was the drug I prescribed. I treated both cats with the medication. The rationale for this belt-and-suspenders approach was that the medication should make the aggressor less aggressive and the victim less anxious (and thus more confident about standing up for itself). Two days into the program, one of this client's cats managed to escape at feeding time. She watched in horror as the two cats made a beeline for each other, but when they reached each other the result was amicable greeting behavior and some mutual grooming before they curled up together to sleep. I wish all these problems were so easy to solve. I have tried the double treatment technique several times since without such spectacular results, but it does seem to reduce hostilities in many cases.

In another case of territorial infighting between cats I completely reversed an attacker-versus-victim situation using two different treatments. It was something of an overshoot on my part. The cats belonged to two veterinary students who shared a house in Grafton, a stone's throw from the veterinary school. The problem started when one of the students moved into her friend's apartment with her cat. The original resident student's cat, Arnold, was the aggressor who patrolled the halls and landings like a hungry lion. The other student's cat, Tammy, was the pariah who had to be confined to her owner's bedroom to keep her out of harm's way—not that she was too keen on coming out anyway under the circumstances. The students had tried graded introductions of the two unwilling cohabitants without success and consulted me for the medical solution to their problem. I suggested buspirone for Tammy, the timid one, to make her more confident, and Prozac for Arnold to make him less hostile. Things did work out along these lines—although the treatments worked too well. Tammy started to explore the house fearlessly and became the lion, whereas Arnold lost his assertiveness and whiled away his time in his owner's bedroom grooming himself and attending to his claws. It was an almost complete role reversal. Talk about listening to Prozac!

Territoriality is a real two-edged sword. You can't live with it, but you can't live without it, even for us humans, it seems. Take the Middle East, the Balkans, or Northern Ireland; people are always fighting for something they believe in. In most cases it's a form of belonging that they value enough to die for. People turn into wild animals if the integrity of their country or culture is threatened. To the uninformed, unthreatened, and unscourged, these struggles appear as sheer lunacy, as in a way they are, but if anyone threatened *your* freedom or *your* family, you would also feel compelled to rise against the oppression and would be applauded for your valor.

In order to inspire dreamers to contemplate a utopian state of brotherhood, John Lennon urged that if we "imagine there's no country, and no religion, too," there would be "nothing to kill or die for." I think he hit the nail right on the head, but the concept is not that practical. In reality—and perhaps it is a mixed blessing—we do have a country of birth, and patriotism and cultural pride are inculcated in us from the moment of our first breath, so until something changes radically, the brotherhood and peace of man has to be brokered.

It's the same for cats. They come from an ancient order of solitary hunters whose best chance of survival is to aggressively protect what is theirs—especially within their territory. Now, a few thousand years later, these perfectly designed, self-sufficient hunting machines find themselves safely coddled in a modern home with an owner who provides for them. In this contrived situation there's no need for the cat to get worked up over where the next meal is coming from, but there are plenty of other reasons for friction between cats, and old habits die hard. Maybe the rift comes over a prospective mate, in defense of young, or because some rude cat has jumped the line for access to a favorite resting spot.

It's amazing, all things considered, that multiple-cat households are as peaceful as they often are. One way this harmony is achieved is through time sharing with regard to access to coveted locations in the home. This quasi-political compromise is scaled down from cats' normal social repertoire in the wild, where territories overlap at the periphery—but correct timing is a vital part of the arrangement. For various reasons such as this, multiple-cat households sometimes exist in a precarious state of balance, with harmony maintained only because of abundant food and a lack of hormones. And it may not take much to upset the balance, as the Pipers found out. Stresses increase as the number of cats in the home increases. Some say that anything over twelve cats in a home is a sure recipe for problems, including territorial aggression. I have seen several multiple-cat households in which the typical "forced" social structure is apparent, with one despotic leader, a stratum of middle-rankers, and a victimized pariah cat. The struggles between the despot and the pariah conform to the definition of territorialism. In nature, the pariah would be driven away, a solution that some behaviorists endorse for domestic frays. But sometimes even these difficult situations can be defused, to some extent at least, by a little environmental manipulation. In one case with which I dealt, the owners of a multiple-cat household compounded a preexisting despot-and-pariah situation by keeping all the litter boxes in the cellar. The despot would sit by the cellar door and attack the pariah every time the poor creature descended from its safe haven upstairs to use the litter box. This cat had to run the gauntlet, with a full bladder, every time nature called. It didn't take much to figure out that an upstairs litter box would make life a lot less stressful for the pariah. That the cat didn't start to urinate on an upstairs rug before the new box arrived is amazing. That cat deserved a medal.

Solutions to territorial problems range from relocation to separation (with or without graded reintroduction) and even medication. It would be nice if some of these principles could be applied to feuding nations. I was going to say that it would be interesting to see what could be done by separating antagonistic factions and arranging a graded reintroduction, but now that I think of it, such measures have been employed throughout history: Hadrian's wall, the Berlin Wall, the Great Wall of China, the Mason-Dixon Line . . . need I go on? When viewed from this perspective, international events such as the Olympic games, where people come together for pleasurable interaction, can be viewed as counterconditioning.

Whatever you may think about territoriality, it's here to stay, and it's something we have to work around. Resolving territorial disputes between people, or between cats, isn't that easy. Territoriality is one of those situations in which an ounce of prevention is often more effective than a pound of cure. Nevertheless, when territorial disputes arise, as they will, we should handle them utilizing the basic principles mentioned above. One thing's for sure: It's not necessary to give up without the old college try. My vote has always been to give peace a chance.

Three

A Case of
Mistaken Identity

My pager buzzed softly on my belt for the second time in the space of a few minutes, summoning me to the consulting room. Unfortunately I was running a little behind, but my new resident, Dr. Jean DeNapoli, had started the consultation for me, so all was not lost. I hurried to the consulting room recalling that the subject was an aggressive cat, but that was the extent of my briefing.

By the time I got to the room the interview was well under way. The first thing that struck me as I crept through the door was the relatively large number of people inside the room. The two owners of the cat were seated side by side at the far end of the room; Jean was sitting at my desk, flanked by a pair of second-year veterinary students; and a postdoctoral research fellow, Dr. Uchida, was positioned by the back wall. There wasn't a chair for me, but I wasn't about to leave to get one, so I resigned myself to chairlessness and slid down the wall into an uncomfortable half squat. Because I was late, I decided to hang loose for a while and see what transpired. I heard something about the fact that the cat was extremely nervous and had never liked other cats. While I waited for a clearer read on the situation, my gaze found a cat carrier with its door shut on the opposite side of the room. I could just discern that there was a tabby-and-white form pressed tightly against the back of the carrier. This was my first glimpse of Miranda, a ten-year-old spayed female domestic shorthair, the subject of everyone's attention and the reason for the assembly. Just as I began to wonder why Miranda was still incarcerated, Jean brought me up to speed with the proceedings, introducing me to the owners, Linda and Michael Smith. Linda was about twenty-five years old and quite serious-looking. As she turned toward me I noticed tears welling up in her eyes behind her slightly oversized spectacles, and I realized that there was a lot riding on this visit. Her husband, Michael, was also intense and seemed to share her concern.

I learned that Miranda had attacked Linda viciously on two occasions, once nine days earlier when she saw a neighborhood cat through the window, and once a short while after this when she heard Linda's sister speaking in a loud, high-pitched voice on the answering machine. Miranda had become extremely agitated preceding her attacks on Linda, hissing, spitting, and puffing up to become her largest and most intimidating self. She had reacted similarly on a few other occasions when confronted with novel situations and certain strangers. She had always been a flighty, skittish cat but had become much worse since the most recent incident. The Smiths were very concerned about Miranda because they cared for her deeply, but Linda had been frightened by the attacks and was also concerned for her own safety.

Jean informed them of her provisional diagnosis and began to outline a plan of action.

"Miranda may be showing redirected aggression," she began.

"This is one of a few possible reactions to an extremely arousing aversive event. The only options for an animal when threatened or challenged are fight, flight, freezing, or redirection of an attack. The window ledge situation you describe, seeing an intimidating sight outside but being unable to attack it directly, is a fairly classic provocation for the redirection response in cats. Miranda redirected her animosity at you and now probably associates you with the terrifying experience. Perhaps when she heard your sister's voice on the answering machine it reminded her of your voice during the encounter. I bet you screamed when you were attacked."

"I did," Linda said, nodding.

"There is one proviso, though," Jean continued. "Although the pattern of Miranda's response is typical of redirected aggression, underlying medical conditions must be considered when an older cat such as Miranda suddenly starts behaving differently. Brain tumors, for example, can cause aggression and personality changes. As a precaution, I would like to do a physical examination and run blood tests to check for systemic problems before pursuing a behavior program in earnest."

Linda and Michael began to look extremely concerned. This talk of brain tumors had really thrown them for a loop. I agreed with Jean about the remote possibility of some covert medical underpinning for the aggression but thought that I should step in to put things into perspective for the Smiths. I asked if Miranda could be let out of her carrier so that we could see her in action.

"I really think it would be unwise to let her out," Linda said nervously. "She's very upset about being here, surrounded by strangers and in an unfamiliar place. I think she would just hiss and spit, and she might even attack someone."

Trying to rule out medical possibilities with Miranda in the carrier was going to be impossible, but I decided not to push it for

the time being because Linda was obviously quite distraught at
the prospect of being confronted by Miranda. It was time to talk
this thing out.

"Dr. DeNapoli's first suggestion, redirected aggression, is the
most likely explanation for Miranda's behavior. Redirected aggression is fairly common in cats, and you have described some of
the typical circumstances that elicit it. Add to that the fact that
Miranda is rather high-strung and you have the perfect setup for a
behavioral problem. Anxious cats are particularly likely to redirect
aggression when confronted with some provocation. They can
turn into Halloween cats at the drop of a hat, their feet gathered
closely beneath them, backs arched, hissing and spitting wildly,
and will divert their frustrations onto anyone nearby. It just so
happens that you were right there the last couple of times Miranda became agitated."

Linda and Michael looked at each other and then back at me.
They were still wary and their expressions told me that they were
skeptical we could do anything to help them. I decided to tread
water with them for a while and proceeded to describe another
case of redirected aggression that was resolved without too much
effort on the owners' part.

The case involved a skittish young adult male neutered cat
called Tigger. One day Tigger's owner, a woman in her thirties,
had a visit from a friend who had just returned from the hospital
following the delivery of her baby daughter. The women chatted
with each other in the hall and then moved into the bedroom,
where the new mother laid her infant on the bed. Tigger crept
into the room with them and appeared to be following them
around. As they fussed over the baby he jumped onto the bed
and began to puff up and hiss. Tigger's owner took quick action,
realizing that something was terribly wrong, and hurried her
friend, baby and all, right out of the house, telling her she would

call later and explain. As Tigger's owner walked back into her house she noticed that Tigger looked positively demonic and was advancing toward her menacingly. She walked briskly to the kitchen and armed herself with a broom for self-defense. This trick worked, but she found herself trapped in one corner of her kitchen, holding Tigger at bay with the broom, for seven hours. Finally he slunk off to a quiet corner to brood. The next day things were back to normal, but the woman decided to consult a behaviorist about the problem, and that's where I came into the story.

I explained that the aggression was probably a result of redirected aggression and advised her to try a program of systematic desensitization. The idea was to persuade Tigger that kids weren't so bad. First I asked her to introduce Tigger to older children under pleasant circumstances until he was entirely comfortable in their presence. I explained that this could take weeks. Then a slightly younger group of children was to be enlisted, and so on, until one day Tigger would be comfortable even in the presence of very young babies. Food treats were to be supplied at every step of the way to condition Tigger to associate kids and babies with good things. Also, Tigger was to wear a collar or harness and a lightweight training lead during the desensitization exercises in order to maintain some control over him, and I advised his owner to be ready to apprehend him should he suddenly become unglued. Tigger did not redirect aggression again during or after the rehabilitation process, even in the presence of babies, and I regarded that as a very satisfactory conclusion. Just to be on the safe side, however, Tigger's family always kept an eye on him after that when children were around.

As I came to the end of this story, I could see that Linda and Michael were beginning to look a little more hopeful. One emerging problem, though, was Linda's extreme fear and mistrust of

Miranda. She said that she no longer felt safe around Miranda unless Michael was at home, and she made Michael confine Miranda to the cellar each time he went out. Even when Michael was there Linda carried a plant mister around with her to repel Miranda should another attack threaten. It was going to take a while for Linda to get her confidence back. I had to come up with a plan that would make her feel comfortable, yet the circumstances surrounding Miranda's sudden personality change were not as clearly defined or easy to address as Tigger's.

I started by discussing a desensitization program with the Smiths, explaining how elements of fear and attack combined to produce the behavior. I told them that the classic behavior modification program designed to address such a problem would involve desensitizing Miranda to her nemeses, unfamiliar cats and loud voices. The voices could be recorded on tape and played back to Miranda at progressively increasing volume while she was eating. There were a few logistical difficulties, however. First, for the desensitization program to be effective, Miranda would have to be protected from the initiating causes, cats and high-pitched voices, except when they were presented in a controlled way as part of the program. This was going to be difficult with respect to outdoor cats because the Smiths could not fully block off all their windows. I gave them a few suggestions about how to reduce Miranda's exposure, however, recommending half curtains or translucent screens taped to the windows to stop her from getting too clear a view of her adversaries. I also advised the Smiths to close the door to their dining room because there were French doors in there that opened onto a rear patio. In addition, I told them to move a window-side wingback chair in their living room, as this was Miranda's favorite vantage point from which she surveyed the world outdoors. Finally, we all agreed that it made sense to turn down the volume on the answering machine, completing the list of stimulus-avoidance strategies.

The next issue related to desensitization itself. For desensitization to be effective, the fear-inducing stimuli have to be controllable so that they can be presented at different intensities, ranging from mild right up to a full-blown challenge. This was going to be tricky to arrange with respect to the outside cats, but I came up with a plan by which Miranda could be desensitized to the original offending neighborhood cat, which lived next door. We would broaden the challenge to deal with other strange cats later. I talked of contacting the next-door neighbor and arranging for meetings of the two cats on neutral territory, with both cats in carriers or restrained by harnesses. Linda's face fell.

"But Dr. Dodman, I don't know whether we'll have time to get involved with this kind of program. I don't think that our neighbor would cooperate, anyway," Linda said.

"And what if some other cat comes along and scares Miranda?" Michael added for good measure.

"Your points are well taken," I replied. "Desensitization programs are difficult to arrange under the best of circumstances and are extremely labor-intensive. If you worked with several different cats over a period of time, the hope would be that Miranda would develop a new, friendlier perspective on visiting cats in general. But then again, you could spend a good deal of time training her only to find that she would go into a meltdown at the first serious challenge."

"Is there another way?" Michael asked. "We need a quick solution. I don't think Linda could stand any more incidents like the ones she's experienced already. The program you describe sounds like it would take an inordinate amount of our time, and it doesn't have particularly reliable results."

"That's a fair assessment," I responded. "These programs can work, but they're not for everyone. Also, in Miranda's case, the outside cat problem is a little nebulous and therefore difficult to target precisely."

"So what else can we do?" Linda asked, sounding a bit frazzled.

"We could try medication," I replied. "The right medicine could make her less afraid in a matter of days, and in her new, more relaxed state, she may automatically desensitize to her fears."

"What kind of medication are you referring to?" Michael quizzed. "We don't want to sedate her, if that's what you're talking about."

"No, I wouldn't sedate her," I responded. "That's the bad old way. Nowadays it's possible to calm animals quite innocuously with specific mood-altering drugs."

"You mean Prozac?" Linda asked, surprised.

"Why, yes," I said a little sheepishly. "Prozac or one of its relatives would do the job, but there are other medications to try should that fail."

The two of them glanced at each other and then back at me.

"Listen," I said, "you're in a difficult situation. You can't go on the way you have been going. Linda, you seem to be really intimidated by Miranda, and life is difficult for you under the present circumstances. Behavior modification alone isn't much of an option for you, so the way I see it, you have no choice. You'll just have to trust me to help you or else find a new home for Miranda. If my helping you means medication for Miranda, so be it."

They both agreed that medication was probably the best solution and added that finding a new home for Miranda was not something either of them would ever consider. I realized their dedication to helping Miranda at this point and was somewhat surprised to find out that Michael was at least as committed as Linda. This is not the normal arrangement, as most husbands, if they show up at behavior appointments at all, seem to be along for the ride rather than there because of any primary concern.

Anyway, with our course decided, the Smiths asked for some more information about the medication, in particular how effective it was, and, as usual, I preferred to transmit this information to them by way of a story.

A pertinent case that sprang to mind involved one of my star patients, Rubles, a three-year-old neutered male Abyssinian belonging to Jessica and Peter Goodman from Hartford. Once again the problem was aggression directed toward a family member—specifically, toward Peter. Peter and Rubles were Jessica's two favorite males, with Rubles something of a surrogate son, and the ongoing conflict was taking its toll on her, so something had to be done. Three months earlier Rubles had been a normal though sensitive indoor cat who enjoyed an almost utopian existence. He lacked nothing, or so it seemed. Even the Chinchilla that dines from a stemmed crystal dish in the cat food commercial had nothing on Rubles. Then, one day while Jessica and Peter were out, a cataclysm occurred that resulted in a Jekyll-and-Hyde personality change. Luckily it was witnessed by the cleaning lady; otherwise we might never have known exactly what happened. The event that triggered Rubles's personality change may not sound too terrible to a human, but to a cat it was like the Bay of Pigs invasion. Rubles was hanging around that fateful day, interspersing catnaps with desultory grooming, when suddenly a pirouetting Cocker Spaniel appeared on the back deck. Its spinning antics were in full view through an elegant set of glass sliding doors by the downstairs coffee table. Rubles stared at this big-screen horror, complete with yelping sound effects, and began his Hyde-like metamorphosis in front of the astonished cleaning lady. In the middle of this commotion, the dog's owner, a slim gent with a beard, appeared on the scene and proceeded to spank his dog into submission before Rubles's eyes. Rubles assumed the classic Halloween posture and had a wild look about him. Moments later the bearded man stumbled off, dragging his dog behind him, and peace reigned once more—except in Rubles's mind, that is. Thirty minutes later, when the cleaning lady left, Rubles must have still been ready to repel boarders, judging from the events that followed.

It was two hours later when Peter returned home. He entered the apartment in the usual way and made his way over to the coffee table. Three or four steps into this journey he was attacked by a flying ball of fur and teeth—Rubles. The whole thing was reminiscent of a scene from *Gremlins.* Peter fled upstairs and was relieved to discover that he had not been pursued. Shortly after the attack, Jessica came home to find Peter shaken and confused by what had transpired. During the dialogue that ensued, and by virtue of a phone call to the cleaning lady, Peter and Jessica reconstructed the entire sequence of events, though they remained puzzled by Rubles's turncoat behavior. There were many other aggressive events after the initial calamity. All of these involved Peter and all of them were in the vicinity of the coffee table. The farther Peter was from the coffee table and the window the safer he was. Upstairs there was sanctuary for Peter because Rubles always behaved with the utmost decorum on the second floor.

The local vet ruled out medical causes for the behavior and correctly informed Peter and Jessica that the problem was redirected aggression. He treated Rubles using a combination of avoidance, desensitization, and medication. The medication, an antidepressant called Elavil, was a reasonable selection; however, Rubles continued his attacks, albeit at a slightly reduced rate. In desperation, Jessica and Peter came to see me. I listened carefully to the whole scenario, nodding agreement with their vet's diagnosis. But I also made a couple of additional discoveries for myself. For example, I learned that Peter was also tall and slim and had a beard, just like the man on the deck. Could it be a case of mistaken identity, I wondered? The location-sensitive nature of the problem fascinated me, too, and helped me plan the desensitization program using location as the variable. Before we parted, I advised Peter to avoid the coffee table area when Rubles was around. I did this partly for reasons of his personal safety but also so as not to wreck any improvement we might make with the program.

I weaned Rubles off the antidepressant drug the local vet had prescribed and prescribed a similar but more specific drug, Anafranil, which behaves like Prozac. Rubles was medicated with Anafranil once a day, and his attitude began to change within days. The improvement continued until it reached a stable plateau after three months, and after that Rubles was almost one hundred percent back to normal. Barring a few slight wobbles during the last two years, this progress has been maintained. I did attempt to talk Jessica and Peter into weaning Rubles off medication on a couple of occasions, arguing that he was probably no longer a danger to Peter, but Jessica wasn't comfortable with this suggestion. She asked whether there was any reason Rubles shouldn't continue on the medication, and I had to admit that I didn't know of one. Consequently, Rubles continues on Anafranil to this day and is none the worse for it (actually he's a lot better). I think Jessica had been so shaken by her earlier trauma that she didn't want to find herself back in that situation for all the tea in China.

When I finished my story about Rubles I sat quietly, eyeing the Smiths and awaiting their response. Now they looked more interested than worried. After a brief conference, they opted to go forward with the Anafranil treatment to complement the environmental modification and retraining measures I had discussed earlier. The other folks in the room began to talk quietly on the side as Jean prepared to take Miranda back to the wards for a physical examination and blood sampling. Miranda went quietly and didn't object to either procedure. The Smiths were relieved to get Miranda back and bid us farewell, prescription in hand, promising to call back the next day for the results of the blood work. As anticipated, the blood work was normal, so the treatment was initiated.

But there was a twist in the tale of the Miranda problem. As the weeks went by, there were times when Miranda seemed to be improving, but she never quite settled down. Just when things started to go well, there would be another minor conflagration. On one recheck visit I decided to change Miranda's treatment to see if I could stabilize the problem further. My next choice was an anticonvulsant drug, phenobarbital, because anticonvulsants also have antiaggressive properties. The result was spectacular. Over the next three weeks Miranda's aggression tapered off and there were no more attacks or even close calls. Linda's confidence started to build, and things returned to normal in the Smiths' household. Miranda's amazing turnaround with anticonvulsant treatment made me wonder whether some underlying seizure problem had triggered her initial redirected attack, but without further expensive tests I would never know.

For the time being I have classified Miranda as a case of redirected/fear aggression that did not respond well to antidepressant therapy. I will wait for other similar cases and the opportunity to perform the necessary diagnostic tests before committing to the more nebulous diagnosis. Whatever the correct explanation for her adversarial behavior, the outcome I could honestly pen in the Miranda file was extremely good for all concerned.

When cats such as Miranda, Tigger, and Rubles redirect aggression toward a family member, life can become quite miserable for the family, as we have seen. At the root of the problem of redirected aggression is aggression that does not have an appropriate outlet. The analogy of an angry man punching a wall is a good one. In fact, punching walls is also a form of redirected aggression. I once heard of a dog attacking a horse every time a car pulled into the driveway. What else but redirected aggression? The dog's real concern was the car, but he was afraid to attack the car, so the poor horse came in for it. Another dog ran half a mile to attack its sibling whenever it received a shock from an electric fence, and yet another attacked its sibling every time someone rang the doorbell.

Other cats may be the subject of cats' redirected rampages. In fact, redirected aggression between cats is more common than the interspecies variety we have already discussed, and it can wreak havoc in a previously peaceful home. The paradox of this type of feline aggression is that it usually occurs between cats that are mutually bonded or at least quite accepting of each other. Owners sometimes witness the moment when fighting begins, but more often they do not. It is more common for owners to wake up, turn around, or return home to find that their cats suddenly seem determined to tear each other's heads off. The hallmark of this type of redirected aggression between cats is its precipitous onset. I have witnessed the start of redirected aggression between my own cats. Both members of this mother-daughter team are normally so timid that they would probably jump on a chair if a tough-looking mouse appeared. They absolutely dote on each other, and they spend half their lives grooming each other and the other half sleeping entwined like a pair of inverted commas. That's why the whole thing was such a shock.

It was nine o'clock one summer evening. Cinder and Monkey were hanging out by the screen door leading to the back deck, taking in the night air. All of a sudden a strange tom appeared on the deck, and Cinder puffed herself up to what seemed like twice her normal size and then started to emit a continuous low growl.

You would think that she would have attempted to intimidate the infiltrator, but instead she lunged at Monkey, her own daughter, who was an innocent bystander. Within a split second both cats were rolling around in a clinch on the floor of my wife's office, screaming and hissing at each other and literally trying to scratch each other's eyes out. I sprang up to interrupt this wanton savagery and managed to shoo them both through into the dining room, where a standoff ensued underneath the dining room table. By this time, both of them were highly aroused, hissing at each other nonstop, pupils dilated to the maximum, and tails switching angrily. I approached the younger cat, Monkey, in what turned out to be a vain hope that I would be able to pick her up, but this normally calm and somewhat shy cat hissed at me and showed me a mouthful of teeth. I realized that if I intervened I was going to be the next subject of the redirected aggression and decided on an alternative strategy. As shooing had worked so well minutes earlier, I elected to try it again, and I successfully managed to shoo Cinder behind a door leading to the back stairs in my house. By closing an upstairs door, I had her effectively isolated from Monkey, and that's the way I left it for the night. The next morning I came downstairs and, with trepidation, opened the door to the back stairs. Then I walked smartly to the cats' double food bowl and tapped it on the counter, signaling that breakfast was ready. To my great relief both cats came running from different sections of the house and began winding themselves around my legs, murmuring softly, begging for food. Then they both took their places on either side of the food bowl and began to eat as if nothing had happened. That was the end of that, and peace has reigned since that time (knock on wood). In this case, the physician did heal himself—or rather, his cats.

I have heard that if you separate cats immediately following (or preferably before) a bout of redirected aggression the outlook is good for complete resolution of the problem. That certainly was true in this case. However, by the time clients consult with me, the relationship between feuders has often deteriorated considerably and treatment is far from simple. This is how it was with Harriet's three-year-old spayed female cats, Fluffy and Tuffy, who had started fighting with each other after years of peaceful coexistence. Harriet, an elderly client of mine from Berlin, Massachusetts, witnessed the start of the problem that was to plague her and her cats for the next six months. Both cats were sitting on a windowsill, watching the world go by, when a strange cat wandered by unacceptably close. Tuffy became extremely agitated, and Fluffy arched her back and puffed up her tail. Before Harriet could intervene, the two cats were fighting savagely and fell to the floor in a flurry of blows. Whether Tuffy directed her thwarted aggression at the frightened Fluffy or whether Fluffy misinterpreted Tuffy's intentions and attacked Tuffy is difficult to say. Both scenarios would have produced the same result: sudden onset of aggression between two cats, catalyzed by an intruder. Harriet separated her cats reasonably soon after the incident but presumably not soon enough, because whenever she tried to reintroduce them the fighting began again. She became extremely despondent, worrying that nothing could be done, and that's when she found me.

When I saw Fluffy and Tuffy, Harriet had struggled through the cycle of separation and reintroduction several times over a period of two or three weeks, but the result was always the same: more fighting. I explained to her that some things just take time and recommended a more gradual, systematic, protracted reintroduction process over a period of months, not days. I remember that she was disappointed by my projection regarding the duration of retraining, but she took heart in the fact that there was light at the end of the long tunnel and returned home to start the rehabilitation process that day.

The reintroduction process went as follows: First the cats were to be kept in separate areas of the house, as mine were, except for a good while longer. As with the Pipers' cats, I advised Harriet to feed the girls simultaneously on each side of a closed door to make at least some of their periodic cross-barrier encounters pleasurable. In addition, I encouraged Harriet to dream up some other fun things to do with them on either side of the "Berlin Wall," such as petting and playing games, to make them associate more than just mealtime with each other's company. Finally, in a bit of a gimmick, I instructed Harriet to attach two toys together by a piece of string under the dividing door so that when one cat played with its toy the other cat's toy also moved, stimulating a response. This tug-of-war arrangement is another way of encouraging cats to have fun across a closed door. As usual, the cats' environments were to be switched daily to prevent territoriality from developing. The rest of the program was along similar lines to the Pipers' program because at this stage of the game the condition was very similar.

Harriet understood what had to be done and stayed in contact with me over the next four months. At the end of this period, her cats were eating in carriers next to each other, and the door to Fluffy's carrier was at last opened. That was when the trouble started. Fluffy went up to explore Tuffy's cage. Tuffy became defensive, and things went from bad to worse. Harriet separated the cats immediately and called me for assistance. The long and short of it was that we had to begin the process all over again. The second time around I cheated by putting Fluffy and Tuffy on the anxiety-reducing drug buspirone to reduce their apprehension of each other and, I hoped, their aggression, too. I had invested a lot of time in this case, and both Harriet and I were rooting for a much-needed therapeutic victory. While I was waiting for news of Harriet's progress, an article was published in the *Journal of the American Veterinary Medical Association* on behavioral therapy for infighting between cats. The treatment plan for the subjects of this article mirrored the one I had created for Fluffy and Tuffy—and the result was the same as for my first attempt, too. The program blew up in the latter phases of reintroduction and the owners had to start over again. (The report never did state whether the problem was finally resolved.)

The weeks ticked by, and my thoughts often drifted toward Harriet's household. I wondered about her likelihood of success with the girls. Finally news came, and it was good. Actually, it was better than good, it was excellent. Fluffy and Tuffy were back together, buddies again. I was ecstatic and felt that the success was attributable to Harriet's perseverance and, in some measure, to buspirone. It had taken six months, luck, and some good work on Harriet's part to get this problem under control, but it was all worth it.

The case of Fluffy and Tuffy confirmed my suspicion that if early separation is not effective in preventing the development of this condition, redirected aggression between cats can become refractory to behavior modification alone. Finding a new home for one of the cats is the usual tack taken by behaviorists at this stage, but I think there is room for some optimism in these cases thanks to the advent of modern anxiety-reducing medication. This is not to say that desensitization doesn't work, just that it doesn't always work and that the outlook may be better when a combination of behavior modification and medication is employed. I have become much less pessimistic about the outcome of chronic infighting between cats since I have learned more about pharmacologic treatments. I still employ purely behavioral treatments initially in many cases (as I did with my own cats) but am happy to prescribe medication if the cats' owner is in trouble with the program or despondent about the eventual outcome. I have direct evidence that this therapy has saved lives, and that's what keeps me going.

Miranda, Tigger, Rubles, Fluffy, and Tuffy are all alive and

well at the time of writing and all is peaceful in their households—testimony to the success of behavior modification therapy.
Considering the consequences of failed treatment, I am sure cats
would view our program favorably if they had a say, and I know
that owners are always greatly relieved to see an end to such
misery. Unfortunately, treatment such as that described for our
heroes is not widely known, and I fear that many cases of redirected aggression result in placement of the affected cats in other
homes, or worse. It's time for the message to get out that something can be done about these problems. Recurrent aggression
toward owners or between cats is not something you or the cats
have to tolerate, and euthanasia is certainly not an acceptable or
justifiable solution.

Four

The Devil You Don't Know

It isn't very often that the clinicians at our veterinary school get a chance to shoot the breeze with the dean. In fact, a personal phone call from his nibs is something of a rarity. For this reason it was with some surprise one morning that I fielded a call from the dean's personal secretary, who asked me to hold while she connected me with the dean himself, Dr. Frank Loew. I waited patiently, wondering what important matter had prompted this call, and then I heard a click and some papers rustling at the other end of the line and realized that we had been connected.

"Good morning, Nick, this is Frank," he opened. "How are things in the behavior world? You're behaving yourself, I hope?"

I laughed politely, knowing that he really didn't want an answer to either question.

"Let me tell you why I'm calling," he went on. "It's a matter of some importance to me and the school, and I need your assistance. I had a call this morning from a woman called Jane Waring, who is housekeeper to Mrs. Amelia Pike. Mrs. Pike is a wonderful old lady in her nineties, an animal lover and a friend of Tufts. Her late husband, who was a doctor, invented some medical equipment and made a fortune when he sold his company. Mrs. Pike has a lovely home, probably one of the nicest in the Boston area, and lives with her housekeeper and her cat, Jonathan. I have visited Mrs. Pike for many years, explaining what we are striving to achieve at the school, and in essence she has agreed to financially support our endeavors. Here is the problem. Jane tells me that there's something wrong with the cat. It's behaving peculiarly and losing weight, and she wants *me* to run down there and take a look at it for Mrs. Pike. I think it's extremely important for us to help her out in this predicament, but I cannot possibly get out of my commitments for today, and anyway, I haven't made a veterinary house call for years. How is your schedule today? Is there any possibility that you could go as my representative and get a read on the situation? I would want you to give me a complete rundown on your return."

What could I say? "I'm afraid I'm just too busy to help you today—try someone else"? No, that didn't sound too good. How about "OK, I would love to help you"? Obviously the right answer. Anyway, my day was flexible and a jaunt into Boston to help out a wonderful woman would probably be a lot more memorable than just another day at the office. I agreed to go and was informed that I would be accompanied by our assistant dean for development, Brian Lee. I knew Brian pretty well and liked the idea of his moral support during my field trip. Moreover, he had been there before and knew the way.

About an hour later Brian met me in front of the small-animal hospital and we set off in his Volvo. I brought the tools of my trade: a case record, stethoscope, and thermometer. Brian brought his Diner's Club card and we stopped off for a wonderful Thai luncheon on the way (*oh, how the other half lives*, I thought).

We arrived at the Pike residence a little late because of our Asian excursion. The roads had become progressively narrower as we approached our destination until finally we curled left into an obscure drive that led to the fabled home. The setting was idyllic. Trees surrounded a sizeable shingle-clad, gable-ended house with leaded windows and brick chimneys. The home wasn't so much a mansion as it was a welcoming chalet. The car rumbled down the long pea-stone driveway and came to a halt by the front porch. As we clambered out, the front door opened and Jane greeted us warmly. We apologized for being a few minutes late, but she wasn't concerned. She took our coats and led us into the house, chattering about Jonathan's strange behavior. I was half listening, half looking as I gazed around the Aladdin's cave in which I found myself. The walls were paneled with oak and the ceilings were white plaster crossed by beams of imposing proportions. The antique furniture contained within each room was enough to cause quite a stir at Sotheby's, and the oil paintings on the walls looked frighteningly like old masters. I didn't dare to ask. My feet trod silently on Oriental rugs. As we entered the living room, which was set off by a spectacular brick fireplace, I caught my first glimpse of Jonathan, or Baby, as he was affectionately known. He was moving quickly, and I gathered that he was not used to and didn't like company. His sylphlike form slid into the dining room, but not before I identified him as a rather handsome and sleek tabby cat of the domestic shorthair variety. Jane closed the door behind him and muttered, "Good, now we've got him." I began to realize that Baby was a bit of a free spirit as Jane proceeded to explain that she was more of a dog person herself. On a count of three we all entered the dining room and shut the door quickly behind us. This room was even prettier than the others and had windows on two sides looking out onto an elegant back garden; on a third side was a glassed-in porch that faced a

difficulties of restraining him single-handedly, Jane told me that the purpose of my visit should never be disclosed to Mrs. Pike. We would have to concoct some other reason, for example, that Frank had sent me to say hello. Although an animal lover, Mrs. Pike was also something of a fatalist and was not likely to approve of medical intervention that would alter the course that nature intended. I agreed to keep my veterinary activities our secret, comforted by the knowledge that Jane was empowered to make decisions on Mrs. Pike's behalf. As it turns out, the grand old lady was mostly confined to her room and wouldn't need to know or concern herself with what we were doing. I looked at Brian Lee and wondered whether he would be able to help me by restraining Baby because I knew that Jane was not going to be a good cat holder. He was an assistant dean, however, and as I surveyed his pinstriped suit and starched white shirt I came to realize that I was on my own. Slowly a plot came to me. I would try to narrow down the field of escape for Baby by somehow ushering him into the glassed-in porch. Then I would make my move and grab him. I told Jane the plan, and she thought it was a good one. She felt almost certain that if we opened the window to the porch, Baby would jump right through, and she was exactly right. Baby was now cornered within this eighteen-by-eight-foot room, and all I had to do was be his friend. Just in case Baby had a meltdown, I asked for a towel to wrap him in as a last resort.

I opened the door to the porch and slid in, taking up a position on a sofa for a few moments while Baby acclimated to the invasion. To my surprise he didn't move a muscle, remaining at his station on a loveseat at the far end of the narrow room. I felt a physical examination was necessary because of his age and weight loss, even though Jane had suggested that Baby's behavior might be attributable to a sort of cabin fever resulting from his cloistered existence. Some cats that are confined and do not have much outlet for their energies engage in daily fits of the "maddies," often around teatime (as we British say). I resigned myself to going ahead with the physical examination anyway and told myself I would take it from there.

I rose from the sofa and walked slowly toward Baby with my hand outstretched. Baby remained on the loveseat and permitted me to approach and sit down. Feeling a little like a member of the bomb squad on a mission, I put a hand under him and steadied him from the side as I lifted him gently onto my lap. I noticed Brian and Jane peering through the windows with mixed expressions of astonishment and admiration on account of the lack of resistance offered by the mercurial one.

I proceeded to lift Baby onto a small drop-leaf table close by and tentatively began the examination. First the mouth, the entrance to the body and revealer of many secrets. I gently tipped Baby's head back, allowing his lower jaw to fall open, and peered inside. To my surprise I did find some things to report. First, the inside of Baby's mouth was not a healthy pink color; rather, the gums were bluish. That was an extremely worrisome finding suggestive of heart disease or lung disease. Now it was particularly important that Baby not get upset and start struggling because exertion can have extremely detrimental effects on a cat compromised in this way. Second, I found that Baby's teeth were covered with tartar and in urgent need of attention. I mused on these findings and moved on to the second phase of my examination, auscultation of his chest with my stethoscope. The lungs sounded fine, but the heart was making a whooshing sound with each beat. I had discovered a cardiac murmur, and considering the bluish appearance of Baby's gums, it was now evident that he had a serious cardiac problem. The rest of the examination, which he tolerated patiently, was unremarkable, but I had already found enough to formulate a hypothesis and suggest a tentative diagnosis. The combination of behavioral change in association with the cardiac condition in a cat of Baby's age was highly suggestive of hyperthyroidism. In this condition, the thyroid glands produce excess hormone, speeding up the cat's metabolism and activity level and resulting in an increased appetite and weight loss, as well as notorious feistiness.

Jane and Brian noticed that I had finished my work and entered the porch. I explained what I had found, and Jane was thrilled with the idea that Baby could now be treated for his aggressiveness.

"So where do we go from here?" asked Brian.

"It'll take a blood sample to confirm the diagnosis," I said, "and it wouldn't be a bad idea to arrange for a cardiac ultrasound examination to see just how extensive the cardiac involvement is."

"Can you do that here?" Jane requested. "You see, we could never bring Baby to the hospital. Mrs. Pike would be sure to notice that he was gone."

"We can't do it now," I replied, "because we haven't got the equipment with us, but I might be able to organize a visit from our cardiologist, Dr. Rush, before too long."

"Would you, please?" Jane pleaded. "I would hate to see anything happen to Baby. It would have a terrible effect on Mrs. Pike."

I agreed to look into it, and Brian and I left, triumphant, for what turned out to be a leisurely drive home to the real world. We never did see Mrs. Pike because she was taking a nap at the time we left, but I did look forward to meeting her at a later date.

A week or so later, Dr. Rush paid Jane a visit and managed to collect blood and perform the cardiac ultrasound examination with Baby under light sedation. The diagnosis was confirmed and treatment with an antithyroid medication was instituted. A few weeks later I called Jane to see how things were going. She was tickled pink with Baby's progress, and he was a little more in the pink, too. His behavior and appetite had returned to normal, and she expressed extreme gratitude to the entire team for the timely intervention that she felt sure had saved Baby's life. It was a good moment for all of us.

I went out to the Pike residence one more time after that, to assist with the dental work I had recommended. This time I was visiting in my other capacity as anesthesiologist as well as providing moral support for Jane during the harrowing anesthetic period. After all we had been through, it would have been a real tragedy to lose Baby to anesthesia, and Jane knew it would never be possible to explain the loss to Mrs. Pike. Fortunately, as usual, all went well and I was delighted to find during the preanesthetic physical examination that the cat's cardiac murmur had disappeared as a result of his treatment. My reward for this excursion was a visit with Mrs. Pike herself (keeping the reason for my presence a secret, of course). I was introduced as Dean Loew's representative, who was in the area and had stopped by on his behalf.

I must admit that as I entered the room I expected to see someone ancient and decrepit, perhaps in a wheelchair, but instead I saw an elegant, refined woman standing before me. She looked like a film star from a Bogart movie.

"Do come in and have a seat," she said. "I don't get many visitors these days. It's very good of you to come."

I did as I was bid and made myself comfortable. Then she perched herself on the edge of her turned-down bed and began to speak of her life.

"I have loved animals all my life," she led off, "and I have always tried my best to help them through philanthropy. It's strange, really, that I haven't been more directly involved with them, but I've had a very busy life, especially when my husband was alive. We went everywhere and did everything together. I do have Jonathan to keep me company, though. He means a great deal to me. If ever anything happened to him, why . . ." Her voice petered out and she began to look around.

"Where is Jonathan, anyway?" she asked. "Have you seen him?"

"I saw him downstairs sleeping," I replied honestly.

"Oh, that cat, he's never around when you want him," she said, and continued with her memoirs.

A narrow escape, I thought.

I listened in wonder as she narrated story after story. I learned about her late husband's life, their adventures together, and more about her passion for animals. I would have loved to have told her about Baby but was sworn to secrecy, which made me feel a little uncomfortable, even though supposedly it was for the best.

At the end of my audience, Mrs. Pike looked directly at me for some time. Then, speaking slowly and deliberately, she said, "You have kind eyes. You *do* understand, don't you? I can tell."

Her penetrating gaze made me feel that she was reading my mind. Luckily, I was thinking only good thoughts at the time! I admired her because of who she was and could only imagine what marvelous experiences she had had. At the same time I was so sorry to see her trapped, as it were, within a failing frame. She was so serene and accepting of her situation. She had no complaints and knew that she had been much luckier than most. I found it almost incomprehensible that the woman in front of me had been a member of high society from about the 1930s on and had moved in the circles of the greats—famous politicians, film stars, authors, artists, poets. She had sipped champagne with them all, and there she was confined to her room with a nurse watching out for her. It seemed like a cruel fate, but the truth is that her whole life, including the latter years, had been close to idyllic. To have had a film-star-like life, to be healthy, wealthy and wise, and to live to be nearly a hundred years old really isn't that bad a deal when you think about it.

I looked at my watch. Time had passed quickly because I had been so enthralled, and it was now time for me to take my leave. Jane had warned me that Mrs. Pike could expend only so much energy at one time and cautioned me not to allow her to overtax herself. I stood up to leave, thanking her very much for the pleasure of her company.

"You will come back and see me again, won't you?" Mrs. Pike asked.

I gained a lot from my experiences at the Pike residence. I rediscovered the importance of performing a thorough physical examination; had a classic reminder of the link between medical conditions and behavior problems; and met an exceptional person whose charisma was still burning strong at the age of ninety-something. She must indeed have been an impressive woman in her youth.

Several other medical conditions can masquerade as behavior problems. I once missed such a diagnosis, but in fairness, it was a tough call from where I sat, fifty miles from the patient. The owner of the cat in question was another elderly lady, Mrs. Blake, who lived on Cape Cod. She called up our behavior hotline seeking advice about her six-year-old pure white split-eyed cat, called Casper. My assistant recommended that she make an appointment, but she didn't drive and couldn't afford the fee, so I decided to try to handle the case as a telephone consultation. I found out during our conversation that Casper, a neutered male, would often bite her while she was petting him. I asked a lot of questions about Casper and about the problem, but none of her answers put up any flags for me, and I diagnosed what seemed to be the most obvious explanation for his misbehavior: petting-induced aggression, or what I now believe is part and parcel of a syndrome of dominance. My advice to her was designed to deal with this problem by avoidance: learning to read the warning signs—the twitching tip of the tail and sideways glances—and bailing out at the first hint of trouble. At the end of the consultation I asked her to call me back in a couple of weeks to let me know how she was doing.

Two weeks later to the day she called me back, as requested, with a good report of how she and Casper were getting on. Apparently Casper had not bitten her at all while being petted because she had effectively rationed his petting and had learned to spot the telltale premonitory signs during what were now less frequent petting bouts. There was, however, still some aggressive behavior in evidence at other times, but I couldn't get a clear picture of what prompted it, and in the end I attributed it to dominance. What I failed to realize was that Casper had started his antics only a year or so before. Dominance would have been in evidence from around the time of puberty, some five and a half years earlier. Because I had failed to register this important piece of information, my advice was to continue with more of the same and then to check back in a few weeks.

Mrs. Blake wasn't the next person to call me about Casper, however; it was her local vet, who had referred her to me. A couple of months had passed since the last news about Casper. The vet was most gracious and nonjudgmental as he told me, for informational purposes only, that Casper had recently started to circle in one direction, probably as a result of a brain tumor. I had a sinking feeling as I heard this news and knew that I had misdiagnosed the problem. Many times it is possible to diagnose successfully across the miles, but there are times when there is no substitute for actually seeing the patient, and this was one of them. Perhaps if I had seen Casper, I might have noticed that his pupils were different sizes, that he had a head tilt, or maybe that he was circling even at that time. Nowadays when I do remote consultations via our Petfax service I always rely heavily on the local veterinarian to screen the patient for conditions I would never be able to pick up on from a fax. This triaging works well, and fortunately I have not made such an error since.

Another possible but unlikely diagnosis that behaviorists need to bear in mind when dealing with aggressive animals is rabies. Rabies vaccination is almost foolproof protection against this killer disease, but vaccination failures are known, and one can never be too careful. The primary suspects for rabies are strays and feral animals with unknown vaccination histories who are brought in from the wild and then start acting peculiarly. Quarantine and observation are required for such animals. It is too risky to take any chances.

Other conditions that cause weird behavioral signs include partial seizures, thiamine deficiency, sugar diabetes, and advanced hepatic or renal disease. Partial seizures display themselves in many different forms, but muscle twitches, agitation, and fits of aggression are the usual manifestations. Historically, partial seizures with their sometimes delusional sequela have been interpreted as possession by evil spirits. Apparently Adolf Hitler had this problem, although in his case possession may have been a more appropriate explanation. Thiamine deficiency in cats, resulting from an all-fish diet, may also produce behavioral changes of mania and unusual skin sensitivity.

The message to take home from all this medical talk is that it is a really good idea to let your veterinarian take a look at your pet if it is behaving strangely. If your cat is spitting at the neighbor's cat or chewing up your plants, chances are nothing is awry medically, but it never hurts to check. I've learned my lesson the hard way and now have a much greater appreciation of why the expression "to vet" has come to mean "to examine carefully." When your patients don't talk, you don't have any other options.

Five

Play School

Several times a year I get a call from someone who claims that their cat is psychotic. Inquiry usually reveals that the cat is immature, an only cat (or at least one without company of the same age), and spends all its time indoors. On further probing, it turns out that the "psychotic" label has been applied because of what are seen as sudden, inexplicable mood changes coupled with paroxysms of owner-directed aggression. Hapless owners try to dodge the hail of claws and needle-sharp teeth but invariably end up covered in scratches or bite wounds. Shouting "no," trying to push the cat away, or attempting to withdraw hands or feet from the battle scene incites the cat even further, as a flailing owner makes an even more exciting target. Exasperation sets in, and the owners search in vain for an explanation for the craziness. "Jekyll-and-Hyde," "possessed," "demonic," "schizophrenic," and "psychotic" are a few of the descriptions I have heard applied to these *Terminator*-type cats.

There are two common patterns of this aggression. In one, the cat shows sudden, escalating aggression directed toward the owner's hands, often following a bout of petting. This aggression takes the form of biting or clawing the petting hand as if the hand were an adversary with a life of its own. Sometimes things get so intense that the cat throws its whole body into the fray and becomes appended to the horrified owner's forearm with its ears flattened to its head and its eyes flashing, looking for all the world as though it's . . . well, possessed. Alternatively, the perpetrator may lie in wait for the unsuspecting owner and spring out to attack the owner's feet and ankles as he or she rounds a corner or steps out of the shower. From the owner's perspective, *psychotic* may seem to be an appropriate term to describe the personality of cats displaying these apparently mercurial mood swings, but the true explanation is much simpler. It is play—only sometimes the owner is the target and things get a bit out of hand.

Everyone who has been around kittens has seen them running around together like young idiots, setting ambushes, springing out on each other, and rolling around on the floor in a series of clinches. We've all seen them chasing around the house, darting and switching direction in an instant, with the pursuer becoming the pursued in this energetic game of tag. Sometimes it's hard to believe that the kittens will ever be friends after these spats, but minutes later the contestants are often found curled up together sleeping peacefully. Play is never taken seriously by the players— that's one of its hallmarks. If it does become serious, it ceases to be play.

Play involves random but fragmentary sequences of normal behavior with the various components repeating themselves at random. Not knowing what is coming next from your opponent seems to be half of the fun. For years experts thought that play was simply a recreational behavior that young animals (and children) engaged in while they were waiting to grow up. That might be true, but then again, there may be more to play than meets the eye. There is evidence, in certain species at least, that play has an important role in normal development and is a necessary part of the serious business of growing up. One of its chief functions appears to be in the rehearsal and refinement of life-sustaining adult behaviors, such as hunting and self-defense. During play, both the mind and body are given a workout, and critical lessons are learned as a result. Strength and coordination are enhanced by play, and it may assist in the fine-tuning of important behaviors. Cats denied interactive play may be less well equipped socially than group-raised counterparts, although this has yet to be proven scientifically. The long and short of it is that play may be more important than we think. We should probably recognize it for what it is and what it means, encourage it, and channel it appropriately.

One report describing the play behavior of group-raised monkeys starkly brings home the message of the importance of play. In this report, all of the play behaviors shown by developing rhesus monkeys were graphed out from birth to young adulthood four years later. There were curves describing, amongst other things, the rise and fall of play fighting and mounting. The monkeys indulging in these behaviors grew up to be normal adults and displayed normal species-typical social and sexual behavior. Monkeys that were raised in isolation, however, without the benefit of interactive play became dysfunctional, directing their escalating drives inward. The result: inappropriate social behavior and self-mutilation.

The lack of social interaction during the formative years may have deleterious effects for human infants as well as animals. Appropriate play in children appears to bring with it all the social and physical benefits described for animals and appears to enhance cognitive and social abilities in later life. In plain English, whoever or whatever you are, play makes you smarter and better-equipped to deal with life.

The other day I was sitting in my office when a second-year veterinary student, Gail Laviolette, poked her nose around the door and asked for some advice about a six-month-old kitten that she and her roommate, Pam, had recently adopted. The problem was that Sam, an unneutered orange-and-white shorthair, would attack them while they were petting him and wouldn't take no for an answer. It all sounded painfully familiar. Sam would jump up on their laps, as cute as a button, and when they obliged by petting him the trouble would start. First would come the shifty sideways glances, then the tip of his tail would start twitching, and then there would be a halfhearted bite or two. The progression from there was rapid, until within minutes Sam turned into a seething mass of claws, teeth, and fur. He didn't inflict any life-threatening injuries during these fits, but he certainly left his mark. Gail rolled up her sleeves to show me some of the battle scars. It looked as if she had put her arms down a garbage disposal lined with steel wool and barbed wire. Sam was also a morning nose biter. Gail and Pam needed help all right, because Sam's play aggression appeared to be leading to the development of alpha cat syndrome and would possibly cause trouble in years to come.

I drew a breath and prepared to explain what to do about the problem, but Gail continued with yet more tales of Sam's antics. It seemed that Pam's ankles were another favorite target for the kitten's aggressive attentions, and this was an even thornier problem. Sam would lie in wait for Pam and pounce at her ankles with the ferocity of a rabid raccoon whenever she headed for the bathroom. This behavior had become so troublesome that it had reduced Pam to tears on more than one occasion and left her with scratches and scars on her feet, ankles, and calves as unwanted souvenirs. Pouncing on Pam's feet while she was in bed was another manifestation of Sam's playful predatory behavior. This wasn't painful as long as her feet were under a blanket, but when the blanket slid to one side, leaving the feet protected only by a thin sheet . . . watch out. All this antagonism didn't prevent Sam from being affectionate to Gail and Pam at times, but that didn't make them feel any better as the attacks escalated from desultory beginnings to a frequency of about ten times per day.

Gail and Pam did have a couple of other cats, but the others were neutered female senior citizens who spent most of the day catnapping and dreaming about the past. They weren't sufficiently animated to be good sparring partners for Sam, and they would usually make a quick exit when he got fired up. The only role they played in his development was as the mortified recipients of his sexual play behavior. When they ran he would chase, pounce, and bite and hold them by the neck. It wasn't bifocals that Sam needed but "the snip." His hormones were beginning to run his life and ruin theirs. This plus the fact that he had sprayed a couple of times accelerated his inevitable fate, and the appointment to fix him was scheduled for that very day. Having commissioned this overdue first step, I began to deal with some of the other issues.

"The aggression toward you and Pam falls into the category of play behavior," I led off. "There are two types of play going on here. One is social play and the other is predatory play behavior. Social play is what you report as petting-induced aggression, with the nose biting being a dominance-related extension of that. The predatory play behavior is the other type of aggression, the one directed toward Pam's feet."

"I thought that's what it was," Gail said, "but I just wanted to hear it from you. So what do we do?"

"As far as the social play and developing dominance is concerned, it is important to set limits and strictly ration your attention to Sam. Do not allow him to muscle his way onto either of your laps whenever he feels like it or to get his back rubbed on command. Pet him occasionally and for a short time only, preferably when he's done something to deserve it. At the first signs of any wildness say 'Ouch' loudly and stand up and walk away. Also, I would keep him out of the bedroom for a few weeks and make him work for his food. Have him come to you when you give a signal, such as tapping on the can of food, and tell him to wait for a few seconds before praising him and putting his food down. He must learn that he can't have whatever he wants whenever he wants it. You might think that sounds a bit tough, but it is no more than you would expect from a well-behaved child who waits for everyone to be seated before digging in. And by the way, don't overfeed Sam. That way he will always be ready to eat."

Gail sat scribbling notes. I cleared my throat and started on problem number two.

"Predatory play behavior is related to Sam's developing need to chase prey or, in this case, prey facsimiles—Pam's feet—as part of his normal development. It is important to recognize that the leaping and pouncing he exhibits is an expression of this need and that it should be channeled appropriately, not prevented. To do this you will have to redirect Sam's predatory attentions away from yourselves and onto other targets, for example, toys. Realize, however, that movement is an essential component of any respectable prey, and that stationary objects, such as toy mice, won't inspire him very much. To introduce motion into the equation you have to be creative, but let me give you a couple of ideas to get you going.

"First, there's the old fishing pole trick, in which you tie a line on a fiberglass fishing rod and attach a leather bow, toy mouse, or milk bottle top to the end. Every morning and evening, or whenever Sam gets into a wild mood, get out the pole and dance the bow around in front of him for five or ten minutes. Drag it across the floor, around corners, up and over the furniture, and so on. Many cats will literally seize the opportunity for this type of play and will leap at, pounce on, and attack the object until they are exhausted. Other ways of achieving the same result that do not necessitate your active participation include attaching the fishing pole to a door or wall, with the target dangling a foot or so from the floor. With luck, Sam will periodically bat at the object and discharge some of that excess energy. Ping-Pong balls and hollow balls with bells inside, which can be purchased from any pet store, can also help provide appropriate play for a would-be hunter, especially if the floors are smooth and level. Sometimes baiting the toy with catnip can get the kitten interested in the first place. Sam should eventually grow out of the behavior, or at least it should fade into relative obscurity, but that may not occur until he is one and a half to two years old, so we need to take action now."

Gail nodded her enthusiastic agreement with this sentiment. She was smiling at the thought of employing some of these ideas, but then a frown came across her face.

"What about punishment?" she asked. "I know that in general you're against punishment, but would it do any good to spank him if he still continues to bite us?"

"Spanking is no good. You could try some slightly less personal deterrent, however, such as shaking a can filled with pennies or spraying him with water from a plant mister the moment he initiates an attack.

"One other thing you could do, which might sound a little radical, is to get another kitten of approximately the same age for him to play with. You might think that having another kitten would double your problems, but it may actually eliminate them entirely. Sam and the new kitten would be able to blow off steam together, freeing you up to carry on with your lives unimpeded. It's like having neighborhood children around to play with an only child. The peer provides company and entertainment and diverts the child's attention from the parents."

Gail looked a little doubtful about this suggestion, but she made a quick note of it and then looked up.

"All right, I think I have enough to work on for now. I'll go back and explain all this to Pam. She'll be relieved to hear that Sam isn't crazy and will be even more relieved if we can get him to stop attacking her feet. Thank you for your time. I hope you don't mind my calling you up in a couple of weeks to let you know how he's doing."

"No, I don't mind. In fact, I insist," I replied. "I always like to know how my advice works out. Without feedback I would never learn myself."

As she left I wondered which of the suggestions would prove most helpful for her and looked forward to hearing back about her progress. A few weeks passed before I heard from Gail again, but eventually the call did come.

"Dr. Dodman, I have some news for you," she said in an encouraging tone.

"Let me have it," I replied, "I do hope it's good."

"I think so," she chirped. "First of all, we did have him fixed, and it seems to have cooled his jets regarding attacks directed at the other cats. Also, I believe he's a little more mellow. We did what you said about rationing his petting, and it's worked like a charm. When we see the tip of his tail start twitching, we just stand up and walk away, and if he follows us, the spray bottle treatment has proven effective. Keeping the bedroom doors shut has helped us avoid his morning antics and, I think, sent him a message that we're serious. Another thing that has gone well is the training. We have finally trained him to sit for food, and I think he respects us for it. We used the click-and-treat training method. First we stood in front of him and waited for him to sit. Then, when he did eventually sit, we would immediately click the clicker and put his food down. Now he has it down and follows us around as we fill the bowl, waiting for his opportunity to perform. I think he actually likes to work to earn his food. His springing out and attacking our ankles has virtually ceased. I attribute that to our playing with him using a feather, a milk bottle top, and a Ping-Pong ball. We attached the first two to a fishing pole and have played chase with him every morning and evening since I saw you. He loves the feather. The Ping-Pong ball seems to be his nighttime favorite, though, because we hear him batting it around after we've gone to bed. We weren't going to get another kitten because we were so upset by his earlier behavior but now we might, just for fun, and of course to get him a friend of his own age to play with. You see how far we've come!"

"I do," I replied. "I think you've cracked the problem, and the really good news is that now you'll be able to help kitten owners who come to you with the same problem. There's nothing like actually working through a behavior problem to its successful resolution to get confidence that you can share. Stay in touch."

Several weeks later Gail came to see me again to tell me the latest about Sam's progress, but I was not in my office, so she left me a note.

Dear Dr. Dodman,

I want you to know that Sam is doing very well, although for a while he was still biting occasionally. Also he became a bit antisocial and wanted to be outside all the time—so we got him a kitten. He is getting along with her famously. They play together and groom each other, and all four cats are sharing a large food bowl with no fighting. All *aggressive behavior from Sam has stopped, and he has become quite affectionate toward Pam and myself.*

Thanks so much for your help.
Gail

I was once a victim of play aggression myself, which is probably why I sympathize with the plight of those on the receiving end. It was many years ago, shortly after I graduated from Glasgow University Veterinary School. I was a young intern and had just adopted Bianca, a pure white kitten with cobalt blue eyes. She really was as pretty as a picture. One evening I was relaxing on my bed with a book when Bianca jumped on top of me and started to nose around. It was a heartwarming scene—a man, his book, and his cat. The only trouble was that Bianca's nosing around became a little too literal, as she started to explore my face, my nose, and then . . . ouch! I leaped to my feet as if I had been stung, experiencing a searing pain in my nose. The bite literally brought tears to my eyes. I was initially confused and disoriented. When I realized what had happened, I felt somewhat betrayed by the mite. After all, I had trusted her, but she hurt me. I felt my throbbing nose and found that it was bleeding. *Bianca, you little devil*, I thought. Bianca had been catapulted into the air as a result of my Gulliverian upheaval and was looking a little startled. That was the last of the serious incidents between Bianca and me because we both learned something about each other that day. Bianca learned that if she bit me hard, I would move very fast and shout very loudly. I learned not to let Bianca anywhere near my nose.

The good thing about play aggression is that it is to a large extent self-limiting. Basically it should lessen over time and should not be a problem in, say, a two-year-old cat. This isn't always the case, however, and my wife has an elderly client who has been on the receiving end of some pretty wild play aggression from her cat, which is three and a half years old. A behaviorist colleague of mine attributes this lingering play aggression to early neutering. He feels that cats neutered late (or not at all) rarely engage in play behavior when they reach adulthood because they mature properly and are beyond such antics. Early neutering, on the other hand, produces a Peter Pan syndrome, with play continuing into young adulthood. The jury is out on this one, but it provides food for thought.

In the meantime, play aggression is out there and is best combated in the manner described. I will be interested to follow Sam's progression into adulthood. Will he have learned his lesson permanently, allowing Gail and Pam to relax their guard, or will he continue to push them? My suspicion is that, with his new, firmer handling, he will develop into a fine and affectionate cat, but if he starts up again, he will find himself back in boot camp before you can say "alpha cat."

Part Two

Emotional
Behavior

Six

Haunting
Experiences

The winter of 1989 was an exceptionally busy time for my wife, Linda, and me. We had just moved into an old house that needed a lot of attention, were working full tilt at our various veterinary enterprises, and were preparing for the arrival of our first baby. There almost literally wasn't a spare minute in the day. As we were having dinner one evening she asked somewhat sheepishly, "What would you say to adopting a couple of cats?"

I stopped midmouthful to digest what she had just said. We were both cat lovers but had been catless for a couple of years. The pros and cons of the prospect started to rush through my mind. Having cats around again sounded good to me, but was it the right time in our lives to adopt a cat or two? Would these new additions to the family be happy to be left alone for long hours during the day? Should they be indoor-outdoor cats, or should they be confined to the home? What about the busy main road outside the house? (That thought pretty much finalized the indoor-outdoor decision.) What about toxoplasmosis, that parasitic disease of cats that certainly has to be considered when someone in the house is pregnant? As my Gatling gun mind revolved around the issues, Linda expanded upon her proposal.

"The reason I ask is that there are a couple of cats at the clinic where I work that need a home. They are a mother-daughter pair. The mother was brought in as a found cat with a full litter. All except the mother cat and the last kitten have been adopted. I feel so sorry for her. If her last kitten is adopted, she'll be alone, and if she's not adopted . . ."

There was no need to continue with that thought. The mantelpiece clock ticked noisily behind me as I wrestled for the correct answer. Linda nonchalantly continued her dinner, and I had a strange feeling that the decision had already been made.

"What is the mom like?" I asked.

"She's beautiful," Linda replied. (How did I know she was going to say that?) "She has long jet black fur and green eyes. She seems very sweet, though she's really scared in the hospital. The kitten is cute, too. She's a tabby, about eight weeks old. Doesn't look much like her mom."

I continued to ponder the matter, and Linda, sensing my uncertainty, tried another tack.

"I tell you what," she said. "Why don't I bring them home tomorrow night for you to see? If you like them, we'll keep them, but if not, I'll take them back."

I have heard several different versions of the biggest lie in the world, but this one took the cake. I agreed to the plan, realizing that I didn't have much say in things at this point.

The next day was a killer. My busy clinic schedule erased all thoughts of new cats, and I was relieved to return home for some peace and quiet by the end of the day. I was the first one back and was just opening the mail when I heard Linda's car pull into the drive. A couple of minutes later, after some slamming-door sounds from the direction of her car, the kitchen door opened. I glanced up to see her, white coattails flying, stethoscope dangling from her neck, and a huge cardboard cat carrier in her arms, trying to fight her way past the side door against an overpowering spring—a formidable task for one who was, at that time, eight months pregnant.

"Well, don't just stand there, help me," she said as I froze like a frightened deer caught in the headlights, still trying to fathom what was happening.

As the mental fog cleared I sprang to my feet and held the door while she struggled through with her precious cargo. She deposited the carrier on the kitchen floor and immediately went to the sink to wash up. I stood there staring at the box for a few seconds, listening to the faint rustlings inside.

Oh, well, I thought, now remembering the previous night's conversation more clearly, and proceeded to gently pry open the cardboard flaps. By the time I had the box open Linda was by my side, and we both peered at the innocents inside, which stared back with big eyes. Linda closed the door to the living room so that the new arrivals would not flee and become lost in our maze of a home, and then we just stood around and waited. Before too long mom cat emerged from the box and scurried across the floor with a slinking gait to the farthest, darkest corner of the kitchen, where she took refuge under a cast-iron radiator. The kitten hopped out of the container shortly afterward and, with an air of confident indifference, began exploring the new environment.

"Well, what do you think?" Linda asked. "They're cute, aren't they?"

"The kitten seems fine," I replied, "but mom cat seems a bit skittish."

"She'll settle in," Linda said, and the pair were here to stay.

It didn't take us long to realize that the mother cat, subsequently named Cinder, was deeply mistrustful. More specifically, she was fearful of all mankind, including us. Basically, she never came out from under the furniture and was rarely seen unless she was scurrying from one hiding place to the next. Her kitten stayed close to her and at times was also a bit of an apparition. Some days we could tell we had cats only by the fact that the food we put down disappeared and from the telltale signs in the litter box. Characteristically, Cinder would defecate right next to the box instead of inside it—a habit we recognized as litter box aversion and which we quickly remedied by changing to a scoopable litter. (See the next chapter for more information on this subject.) Anyway, to put it mildly, Cinder wasn't a particularly friendly cat, and we were beginning to wonder whether she would ever straighten out. Linda and I came to the sad conclusion that Cinder had been subject to some kind of abuse, because her fear of people was so great. We didn't think she had been hit, but she may have become mistrustful as a result of undersocialization, neglect, or some other adverse experience. She was, in my terminology, a dysfunctional cat, and her rehabilitation was going to be quite a challenge. The kitten, on the other hand, was quite normal and extremely playful. She was so playful and mischievous, in fact, that she earned herself the nickname of "the monkey," or just Monkey, and that name has stuck till this day.

For Cinder, our thoughts turned to the behavioral conditioning technique of systematic desensitization. During this approach to the resolution of fearful conditions, apprehension is reduced at each level of exposure to the stimulus by avoiding the negative consequences previously associated with it. An even more powerful approach is to arrange for a *pleasurable* association to accompany each stage of the desensitization process. As a prerequisite for successful retraining, it is important that the fear-inducing stimulus be identifiable and controllable. Also, the cat must be prevented from having unmonitored exposure to the fear-inducing stimulus during the entire retraining process. This can be difficult to arrange, and it may be nearly impossible if you aren't sure what is provoking the fear. In this case, Cinder's fear was of people, so we knew what we were trying to desensitize her to. In addition, we felt that we could quite easily modify her exposure to us because her loner lifestyle would prevent sudden rude interruptions and unexpected meetings. In short, we had the essential ingredients for a successful rehabilitation program.

There are two ways of conducting a desensitization program. Either the cat can be brought progressively closer to its nemesis, an active process of reexposure, or it can be allowed to approach at its own speed, the passive approach. I refer to the latter as autodesensitization, but technically it is known as habituation. The active approach requires putting the cat in a wire carrier or restraining it with a harness, so that its progression can be controlled. With the passive approach, on the other hand, no physical restraint is required, and this often seems better-suited to the cat's independent nature. Either process can be hastened along if the graded reexposure to the fear-provoking stimulus is coupled with pleasurable experiences. Highly palatable food is often a powerful ally in this situation.

Autodesensitization was the strategy for Cinder. The actual process is quite simple, though time-consuming. The plan was to wait until Cinder was securely ensconced under her favorite objet d'art in an upstairs sitting room, and then we would join her in the same room and close the door behind us. We would sit down on a couch on the far side of the room, each armed with a good book and a sandwich bag full of cat treats. A most important prerequisite was to make sure that Cinder was hungry before we started our sessions, and we did this by picking up the food bowl a few hours earlier. Hunger is the best sauce, my grandmother used to say. Step one was to allow Cinder to desensitize to our presence from her vantage point under the furniture. We literally just sat there and read, hour after hour, night after night. Prior to each session I would slide a food treat across the birchwood floor, trying to get it provocatively positioned a foot or so from Cinder's retreat. I became quite proficient at this game of cat-treat bowling and before too long could land the temptation in the designated zone virtually every time. It was a sublimely peaceful behavior modification program. The only noise in the room was the occasional rustle of pages. The whole situation reminded me of the many hours I had spent fishing with my dad, just waiting for something to happen.

After a week or so of this vigil, we were rewarded for the first time when a paw came out from under the furniture and the food treat disappeared; this was the first chink in Cinder's defensive armor and the first faltering step she took toward alleviating fear and developing trust. After several weeks Cinder became more confident at various levels of approach toward us. First she would only hook in food treats that landed close to her. Then she would emerge to procure food treats that fell a little short of the mark, although she would scuttle back to safety quickly once in possession of the spoils. Eventually she became almost blasé about retrieval, progressively gaining in confidence to the point where she would take treats from the couch next to us and ultimately from our hands. The latter involved jumping up on the couch, and after that it was only a matter of time before she would sit on our laps to be petted. Thinking back, the whole process took several months, with about a month between each of the stages—confidently taking food from the floor, taking food from the couch, taking food from our hands, and finally sitting on our laps. Without food all of this would have taken a good deal longer.

Getting Cinder used to us was the first hurdle, but there were when unsocialized kittens beyond a certain age encounter people for the first time. This is the blueprint from which feral kittens are made. The responses of the fearful and the feral vary but include avoidance of ominous situations by fight or flight, freezing, and redirected aggression if a target happens to be handy.

Feral kittens present a real problem for anyone wanting to rehabilitate them, for reasons that should now be apparent. These unsocialized cats grow up in the splendid isolation of their own litter, and to them, everybody and everything outside their world is unfamiliar and a potential threat. And potential threats are treated with great suspicion, avoided, or driven away. When you think about it, the natural tendency to have fear of the unknown makes perfect sense for any animal that nature intended to be raised in the great outdoors. A kitten without fear would be easy prey for a predator, and to have to learn who and what is to be feared from experience would reduce the chances of survival dramatically, so developing a mistrust of unfamiliar faces is definitely a survival plus. With cats, there has been less selective breeding than there has been with dogs, and they have also been domesticated for a shorter time, so cats are by nature much closer to a "wild type." In the absence of appropriate socialization and bonding in early life, cats will display an impressive range of wild cat behaviors, and wild cats aren't that cuddly. There are some wild cats on the Galapagos Islands that are descended from the cats of visiting seafarers. Over a few generations these cats have adapted perfectly to their environment and have pretty much reverted to a bona fide wild type, developing into a totally independent breed of slim, trim hunters that survive by eating crickets and lizards. I understand they're not much fun as pets, though.

So is there any way to rehabilitate a first-generation feral cat? The answer is a guarded yes. It depends on how long the cat has been in the wild and on how much time and attention can be put into its rehabilitation. It also depends on your expectations, because a feral cat is unlikely to ever become as well domesticated as a cat that has spent its formative months pleasantly interacting with people. So powerful is the influence of early socialization that a kitten raised with an archenemy such as a mouse will come to believe that the little creature is a buddy, not breakfast. The early learning experience has such a profound effect that it will override the hardwired tendency for the cat to view the critter as prey. If appropriate socialization does not take place, a cat's perception may be altered, but only through a slow and continuing learning process. You can teach an old cat new tricks; it just takes time. Unfortunately, some potential adopters of feral cats do not have the time or patience for this. Unmanaged fear is self-reinforcing, creating a catch-22 situation. The fact that the cat is scared makes it feel bad. This means that the next time the unpleasant situation occurs, the cat has two reasons to dread it, the original one and the memory of the bad feeling it creates. I have sometimes been able to make headway in such cases by treating cats with the anxiety-reducing drug buspirone. One feral cat I treated was converted into an affectionate, outgoing individual after three weeks of treatment. I had the medication withdrawn at this time and the behavioral improvement was maintained, presumably because learning had taken place. I have tried this strategy several times since, and feedback from owners generally has been good.

One of the things feral cats do very well is to hiss and spit at approaching humans. This type of aggression is well documented in the scientific literature and is termed the feline affective defense response or, more colloquially, fear aggression. Every behaviorist worth his salt knows this syndrome well. Affected cats hiss and spit and display a constellation of other signs that advertise their inner turmoil. Signs such as dilated pupils, raised hair along the back and tail, and unsheathed claws are all typical of this hyperaroused state. Arching their backs to make themselves appear bigger, creating the classic Halloween-cat image, is part and parcel of a strategy designed to persuade would-be attackers that their effort may not be worthwhile. If pressed, fearful cats will attack, scratch, or bite the opposition, although damaging the foe is not usually their primary intention. Scratching is more likely than biting in this situation, as any veterinarian who consults without wearing heavy gloves will testify. Biting is more usually the work of confident, outgoing cats that are determined to make their mark on the world. As might be expected, the central theme in the treatment of fear aggression is the same, the time-honored technique of desensitization. This treatment is most effective if the subject of the cat's fear is relatively discrete, for example, the boy next door. Fear that has generalized to large groups of people, such as all adult strangers, is a much tougher proposition and presents problems for the design and conduct of treatment programs. In such cases, medication with anxiety-reducing drugs can be an invaluable supplement.

Fear of people, with or without fear-related aggression, is not the only expression of fear in cats. Like other species, cats can also become scared of sounds, sights, and smells and of certain situations. I see fewer of these fears and phobias in cats than I do in dogs, although this may be due to a reporting bias. It is hard to ignore a dog with thunderstorm phobia, as it paces, pants, and salivates. Some dogs with this phobia even throw themselves out of open third-story windows during a storm if their owners are not there to prevent it. That always seems to get some attention, although attention seeking is not the motive for this dramatic behavior. Also, dogs with separation anxiety are difficult to miss, as their "home alone" anxiety erupts into hysterical barking or, even worse, barrier frustration, in which extensive damage is inflicted upon doors, blinds, and windowsills. Cats with similar problems have much more subtle ways of acting out their fears and anxieties, and consequently their woes are much less likely to come to their owners' attention. Nobody goes to the vet because their cat sometimes hides under the couch or goes for a few hours without eating. I can't recollect ever being consulted about thunderstorm phobia in a cat, but I feel sure that it must occur. Separation anxiety is another condition that often goes unnoticed in cats. Inappropriate urination in the owner's absence may be the only obvious sign of this condition, but even when that occurs, its significance is often misinterpreted. Picking up on fear-related problems in cats is what presents so much of a problem. Once the conditions have been recognized, however, they can be dealt with by the time-honored method for addressing fears, systematic desensitization.

Not all feline anxieties are as cryptic as the ones just described, and some are even quite obvious. An unpleasant experience at the vet's, for example, will make every aspect of the trip to the veterinarian's office unforgettable for a cat, complicating all future attempts to transport the reluctant cat to that or other locations. This avoidance reaction is triggered by many facets of the previous visit, including the sight of the cat carrier, car travel, the smell of the vet's office, people in white coats, the specter of the vet himself, and much more. This fear is difficult to miss. You know that something is wrong when it takes thirty minutes to catch your cat to take it to the vet's for its annual shots, when it vocalizes its disapproval throughout a car ride to the vet, or when the animal turns into a cowering wreck in the vet's waiting room. The solution to this distressing problem is, once again, systematic desensitization. The first step is to retrain your cat to accept the carrier under more pleasant circumstances. Leaving the carrier around with the door open and putting special food treats inside is a good start, as is feeding the cat near and then inside the carrier. The next step is to shut the carrier door for brief periods, rewarding the enclosed animal with food treats for remaining calm and composed. The logical progression is to bring the cat in the carrier to the car, start the engine, and take a short ride around the block. Once this is successfully accomplished you can bring the cat to the vet's and feed it treats in the waiting room so that fear of the destination is overcome. Each step is an obstacle to be circumvented, and the next step can be taken only when the prior one has been successfully accomplished with no associated signs of fear. Finally, the vet must work hard to ensure that all future visits that entail medical therapy are not terrifying or stressful. This requires patience, minimal restraint, and, at some point in the proceedings, counterconditioning. Dentists have this down pat and know that they must treat their patients with kid gloves, even providing sugar-free lollipops for the kids. Retraining your cat to remain calm when visiting the vet's office is all very well, but it takes time and is not particularly useful if you need to take your frightened cat to the vet's tomorrow. For acute situations such as this, there are short-term pharmacologic solutions, such as medicating your cat with a rapidly acting anxiety-reducing drug, such as Xanax. Xanax works quickly and can convert a stressed-out tiger into a little lamb in forty minutes or so. But it can sometimes have a paradoxical effect of increasing aggression, so this is definitely not something to try at home without expert supervision.

Even the signs of separation anxiety are not always as covert as I implied earlier. Tony, a friend of mine from the gym, told me one day between bench presses that his cat vomited on the white wall-to-wall carpeting virtually every time Tony went out. Tony's house-proud wife was just about at the end of her tether because of this problem and the writing was on the wall for his little buddy, who was an extremely handsome though fretful Himalayan called Snowball. From the history, I tentatively diagnosed separation anxiety as the cause of the problem. We didn't have much time for extensive dialogue in the gym, but I told him to try leaving a radio on when he was away and said we would discuss more-detailed treatment options later if necessary. To my surprise and Tony's joy, the next tier of advice was not even necessary because Snowball had quit his antics soon after the radio strategy was implemented. Tony added for good measure that Snowball seemed to prefer country music; this fits right in with what is known about cows, which I am told produce more milk when listening to Garth Brooks.

Some people are just as frightened of cats as some cats are of people. Fear of cats, termed ailurophobia, is as old as the sun and has something to do with that ethereal quality of cats that makes them so mysterious. Even the way they look at a person can be a little unnerving at times. There's something about that fixed, unblinking stare that gives the impression that they are looking right into one's soul. Also the reptilian slitted pupils and the glow-in-the-dark eyes do little to dispel the fears of the fearful. Finally, the cat's propensity for freezing and pouncing, as well as its sheer stealth at night, are unnerving for the uninitiated. I once met a recovered ailurophobe, Gloria, at my father-in-law's house in Washington, D.C. Gloria, now an ardent cat lover, was anxious to talk with me about her prereformation days. Actually, she almost pounced on me when she learned of my interest in cats (I didn't flinch) and told me her intriguing tale. This kind woman had tried to provide a home for shelter cats for years, but each time she adopted a cat and brought it home her own fear overcame her compassion and she had to return the cat within a day or so. For Gloria, the chief problem was at night as she lay in bed listening to the stirrings of a living creature somewhere in the blackness. The final straw would be when the cat jumped onto the bed or the nightstand next to her. When this happened, she would spring up out of bed immediately and turn all the lights on, finding herself shaking with fear and out of breath. The next day she would trudge back to the shelter knowing that she had failed again. The people at the shelter came to know her well over the years and were not surprised to see her again on the day of what turned out to be her first successful adoption. That day she was walking the length of the cattery as usual, peering in this cage and that, when she became aware of a pair of eyes firmly fixed on her. She returned the gaze, coming eye to eye with the prettiest, saddest-looking cat she had ever seen. She knew that this lonely-looking cat had to be the subject of her next adoption attempt. The arrangements were duly made, and the shelter staffer gave a knowing smile as Gloria left clutching her eleventh attempt at adoption.

When she got the new cat home she found the newcomer a comfortable bed, put down food, water, and a litter box, and then attended to some things she had to do. On returning some hours later she found the cat in much the same position as when she had left it. She was worried about this apparent inactivity, bordering on torpor, and summoned the vet. As it turns out, the new cat was sick with some horrible cat virus and needed a lot of nursing attention. Gloria was up to this and felt even sorrier for her pathetic adoptee. It took several days to rehabilitate the new cat, requiring spoon-feeding, patience, and TLC. Of course, one of the features of the illness was that the cat didn't move around much. The first few days of the cat's convalescence must have amounted to a series of long, dreamy catnaps interspersed with periods of deep sleep. The lack of activity, especially at night, allowed Gloria to acclimate herself to the new cat's presence without having to endure the earlier night terrors. The bond strengthened. When the new cat did start to move around, it was not with terrifying leaps and bounds but at a reasonable pace, one that did not instill fear in Gloria. The whole process of this cat regaining its full kinetic repertoire took several weeks, and the process was slow enough for Gloria to adjust to each stage. Without knowing it, she had been on the receiving end of a desensitization program and had overcome her fear. As proof of her newfound courage, she subsequently adopted a second cat. No one was more surprised at this turn of fate than the staffer at the shelter, who just pushed back his cap and scratched his head. He'd thought he had seen it all.

Desensitization is an effective means of alleviating fear in cats and humans, making fearful conditions some of the most rewarding to treat. I often wonder if cats, like people, emerge from their phobias and wonder why they were ever frightened in the first place. That certainly was Gloria's experience. She recovered to the point where her cat's occasional nocturnal perturbations would simply cause her to smile as she realized that there was nothing to fear except, of course, fear itself.

Seven

The Writing on
the Wall

Inappropriate elimination, as it is euphemistically called, is the number-one behavior problem in cats. It refers to the unfortunate tendency of some cats to urinate or defecate outside a designated area in the home, usually a litter box. No other problem causes owners so much grief and leads them so often to consider the final solution of euthanasia. Inappropriate elimination causes a greater loss of cat lives than any other behavioral or medical problem, and until quite recently veterinarians did not have all the answers. If neutering, attention to medical problems, and a course of synthetic progesterone didn't resolve the issue, many of them were stumped for a solution. You can understand the frustration of desperate owners at this point as they find themselves with the choice of living in the atmosphere of a feline latrine or parting company with a good friend. Not such a great choice. Fortunately, information about how to manage such cases has burgeoned of late, and now few cats with this condition would be considered beyond help. Indeed, most can be successfully treated in a matter of days or weeks.

When I started treating behavior problems I was not particularly enamored with the prospect of dealing with the rank-and-file problems of inappropriate elimination. I think my reluctance stemmed from ignorance. I'm sure that if I had been better informed at the time, I would have been more enthusiastic, as I am now. Because of my lackluster attitude, I did not go out of my way to encourage owners of house-soiling cats to come to my clinic, preferring to concentrate my efforts on problems that involved the other end of the beast. It didn't take me long to realize that I had underestimated the challenge posed by inappropriate elimination and the desperate need for effective treatments. As I saw more cases of house soiling, I found that reaching an accurate diagnosis was not always easy and that many of the more complicated problems were quite challenging. Some possessed all the intrigue of a good detective novel, I found, and so I was hooked.

Admittedly, some cases of inappropriate urination are downright simple to diagnose and fix. This is especially true when litter box aversion is behind the problem. Frankie, a domestic shorthair from Worcester, had such a problem, and his case illustrates this point. Frankie's owner, Michelle, called me one day to schedule an appointment for the cat, which had suddenly started to use a rug as his bathroom. During the conversation I asked a few fundamental questions to get a feel for the problem.

"Where exactly does Frankie urinate?" I asked Michelle. "Is it in a dark corner, in the middle of the room, on throw rugs . . . where?"

"Right next to his box," Michelle replied with a sigh. "You'd think he would do me the favor of taking the extra two steps, but no, he has to go on the hall carpet right next to the box. I don't understand it. I keep the box clean for him, scoop it every day, and then suddenly it's not good enough for him."

I was immediately drawn toward a diagnosis of a litter box

problem because of the unflamboyant, stereotypical pattern of the behavior—just missing the mark.

"How long has this problem been going on?" I continued.

"A couple of months, I would say," Michelle answered.

"And was there any event associated with the onset of the problem?"

There was silence at the other end of the phone as Michelle pondered for a few seconds before replying.

"Well, I did put a plastic stair runner underneath his box to make cleaning up a little easier, because he makes such a mess scratching around in the litter. That couldn't have upset him, could it?"

"You bet it could," I responded, realizing that we had hit the jackpot, and went on to tell her a few facts about how cats feel about plastic stair runners. Basically, most cats don't like them. So powerful is cats' dislike of walking on thick plastic that I have used plastic sheeting to deter problem urinaters from soiling a favorite area. Nobody knows why cats don't like plastic surfaces, but it may have something to do with the feel of them.

In sharing this information with Michelle I realized that I had talked myself out of a behavioral appointment at a time when the hospital director was on my back about increasing the caseload. But it didn't make sense to have her come in to hear the obvious next step—to remove the stair runner—so I passed on that and asked her to call me back in a couple of days. If the problem was resolved, as I felt sure it would be, she was off the hook (and so was Frankie). If it wasn't, then I would make an appointment for them to come in. When Michelle called back she reported that the problem had completely disappeared overnight, as antici-pated. She was so thrilled about this that she insisted on making an appointment anyway so that I could meet Frankie and we could gloat together over the successful treatment. And that's the way it happened. We had a wonderful time discussing some of Frankie's other idiosyncrasies and conversing about cats in general. Everyone was satisfied with the conclusion, even the hospital director.

Another case of similar ilk, which for logistical reasons I was handling as a paid telephone consultation, also hailed from the neighboring city of Worcester. The owner of this second problem cat was less cordial than Michelle and was one of those owners who ask lots of questions and then tell you you're wrong when you supply the answers. The situation this woman found herself in was quite intriguing. She had been laid off from work a couple of years earlier and lived alone in an apartment with six cats. Until a short time before her call, all six cats happily shared two litter boxes. She told me she always scooped the boxes each time they were used, so they were always clean and inviting. Then, one day, for no apparent reason, one of the cats started to urinate on the carpet behind the sofa and the woman's life became a nightmare. I suggested that the problem probably stemmed from having too few litter boxes for so many cats. Initially she refused to believe that this could be a factor, reminding me that her present arrangement had been working for years. I understood the point but stressed that two boxes for six cats was a precarious situation—an accident waiting for a time to happen. I suggested to her that perhaps the reason she had been able to make this unsatisfactory state of affairs work was that she was always available to scoop the boxes the moment they were soiled. This intense supervision might have helped avoid problems in the past, even though the litter box arrangements were poor. So what went wrong? I hazarded a guess that one day the offender-to-be wanted to use the facilities while they were occupied and just couldn't hang on. Caught short, this normally well-trained cat would be forced to exercise another option, such as gravitating to that warm, dark place behind the couch. Soiled in this way, the new area would instantly become an alternative "bathroom," with the culprit attracted back to the same spot as surely as a heat-seeking missile zeroes in on a source of heat. The only problem was trying to convince her of this scenario so that I could win her cooperation in the treatment program.

In response to the proposal that she should deploy more litter boxes, she came up with several other less likely suggestions for the inappropriate behavior that did not involve aspects of hygiene and insisted that the litter box arrangements were perfectly fine. As our views were so opposed, the only strategy I could dream up was to challenge her to put down more litter boxes to prove me wrong. She had nothing to lose by following this advice and would have the satisfaction of telling me off if the problem persisted. This win-win situation finally persuaded her that putting down more boxes was worth a try. She agreed to put down two additional boxes for a trial period, although deploying the six boxes I requested (for insurance) was still out of the question for her. As well as augmenting litter box facilities, I suggested a thorough cleanup of the soiled area on the carpet using an odor neutralizer sold in pet stores. I didn't have long to wait for the results. The plot was almost immediately effective, and she called me back just two days later to share the good news. Even though she had lost the battle, she had won the war so admitting defeat over the litter box issue wasn't too difficult for her under the circumstances. After all the wrangling and disagreement, the conclusion of this case was a bit of an anticlimax, but to tell the truth, I wouldn't have had it any other way.

Cats are curious creatures known for their fastidiousness. To them, where to go to the bathroom is almost as important as what to eat. Even the act of going to the bathroom is a kinesthetic work of art, a ballet of semiprogrammed steps and turns. The contented cat enters the box deliberately and spends time selecting just the right location within the box. It then scratches out a small depression in the litter, turns around to position its derriere over the spot, and voilà! All four feet are firmly placed in the box at all times during this skillful maneuver, which apparently takes great know-how and considerable concentration. When the job is done the cat takes time to inspect the fruits of its labor, and then most, but not all, carefully cover up their handiwork, finally hopping from the box nonchalantly to pursue some other activity. When a cat is unhappy with the litter box it is another story. The cat approaches the litter box hesitatingly and without much preamble adopts a squatting position in the box. If it does spend time in the box searching for a clean spot there is usually a great deal of disdainful paw shaking accompanying the activity. It is as if the cat is trying to rid itself of abhorrent material sticking to its paws. A pained expression often comes over the cat's face as it settles down to eliminate, ears back and body tense. Some balance precariously on the sides of the box in an attempt to minimize contact with the litter and end up hanging over the side with consequently ignominious results. And these cats don't hang around in the litter when they're finished. As soon as the business is over they're out of there—no time for scratching around to cover up. Air scratching, rug scratching, and wall scratching beside the box are tokens of a cleanup that doesn't actually happen. The cat just goes through the motions of covering up after itself without actually getting its paws contaminated with the litter. Cats who behave like this in and around their litter boxes are not happy campers, although some still manage to hit the target despite overwhelming odds against this outcome.

Common reasons for a cat's deciding that it doesn't like the litter box include a problem with box location (too exposed or too remote), litter that is too shallow, a box that is too small, the presence of a hood on the box, a box that is too messy or too clean (smelling of harsh chemicals), and, of course, the wrong litter.

Sand-type litters seem to be the ones preferred by most cats, perhaps because cats have desert ancestors and so they have a natural inclination to gravitate toward substances of this type. You only need to have a pile of builder's sand delivered to your back door to convince yourself of this preference. You will quickly find that every cat in the neighborhood will descend on the sandpile to use it as its own personal latrine. The preference that cats have for sand can be really irritating when it comes to children's sand-boxes and is one good reason to purchase a sandbox with a lid. One behaviorist (who must have been between projects) con-ducted the urinary equivalent of cola taste tests to determine which types of litter cats chose. The study demonstrated conclu-sively that sand-type litters are preferred. Most of the sand-type scoopable litters are actually made of clay, so it's not silicon diox-ide per se but texture that holds the attraction. When owners provide previously deprived cats with the sandlike litter of their dreams, grateful cats often dive in with both paws and roll in the stuff in apparent ecstasy. Litter box happiness, it seems, is sand-shaped. Simply changing a cat's litter from rocks to sand is a really effective first step when dealing with inappropriate elimina-tion problems and can sometimes solve a litter box problem in one fell scoop (so to speak).

Only one thing can spoil the joy of sand: perfume. Cats just aren't into perfumes. No self-respecting cat wants to have its sub-tle personal odor masked by overtones of lavender or rose petals. Also, perfumed litters are designed to appeal to the relatively insensitive human nose, so they must seem really pungent to a cat. For these reasons, when attempting to solve litter box prob-lems it is often helpful to switch to unscented litter. Even odors inadvertently applied to the litter box can have a disastrous effect in some cases. Fussy owners who sterilize their cat's box with Clorox or Pine Sol often discover that their efforts have an overall unsanitary effect, diverting their odor-sensitive felines to alternative locations.

People who find that their cat has a house-soiling problem usually take it upon themselves to smarten up in terms of litter box hygiene. I don't very often have to direct my clients to scoop the litter box daily or to change large-particle clay litters weekly. However, sometimes I find that a failure of litter box hygiene in the past has initiated the problem of the present. A typical scenario is that owners go away for a couple of days and return to find the box overflowing and the cat's attentions diverted to another site. Once the inappropriate-elimination problem has been initiated, it is sustained in the new location by the odor of the urine in nonbox locations. Thorough cleanup of the offending areas with bacterial or enzymatic products is an essential part of treatment.

As you may have guessed by now, not all inappropriate-elimination problems are corrected simply by attending to litter box arrangements. There is a whole other category of inappropriate elimination behaviors, which may be lumped together as marking behavior. The most obvious form of this is urine spraying. To spray, cats usually back up to a vertical surface, tread with their back feet, wiggle the tip of their tail, and eject a small spray of urine. There are also horizontal-surface markers who squat and release small volumes of urine for what appears to be a similar purpose. Cats engaging in this type of behavior are not attempting to relieve themselves so much as send a scent message. The message is a form of urinary graffiti designed to inform and ward off would-be infiltrators or advertise one's availability to a potential mate. The usual culprits are males, though females will also indulge under the right circumstances. Neutering will prevent 90 percent of males from engaging in this (to us) obnoxious pastime and will also prevent estrus-linked spraying in females. However, a hard core of sprayers persist after neutering, despite the fact that their hormonal motivation is gone.

But why should neutered cats engage in urine-marking behavior? A good question—and the answer may not be as simple as was originally thought. The classic explanation is that neutered cats that urine-mark are doing it because they are exposed to some kind of environmental stress. It seems that when cats are anxious about something they become insecure and develop a strong need to redefine their territory. They do this using urine (or sometimes feces) as the mark. As disgusting as this may seem at first glance, the practice of sending personal messages through the medium of excretory products is common throughout the animal kingdom. Urination and defecation are much more than a simple waste removal process for most species, and the rituals of who excretes where can be quite elaborate. Stallions always defecate when they meet, and smelling each other's feces seems to provide all sorts of information with various social and sexual implications. Defecation as a method of signaling is so prevalent in stallions that one behaviorist, Dr. Kathy Houpt from Cornell, likes to say that stallions never defecate simply because they need to empty their bowels—there is always something symbolic about it. Still on the subject of marking, some monkeys, goats, and even rabbits urinate on themselves to send a signal in a way that very few of us would appreciate. Excretions can also convey messages remotely; cats are big on this particular cryptic method of communication by marking objects with urine or feces, and therein lies the root of the problem.

Because anxiety is at the heart of much marking behavior, any logical method of treatment should focus on the alleviation of stress. A thorough clinical history is a must, paying particular attention to events that coincided with the onset of the problem. A house plan and daily schedule are also helpful in identifying environmental stressors. The ideal solution is to remove all stressors and improve the cat's environment, but unfortunately it isn't always possible to get a precise read on what is causing the anxiety, least of all do something about it. For this reason pharmacologic agents have been the mainstay of treatment for some years now. Initially synthetic progesterones and subsequently Valium were used, but success was limited, side effects were often significant, and the relapse rate following treatment was high. Progesterone derivatives were effective in only about 30 percent of cases and sometimes precipitated hormonal problems such as sugar diabetes and adrenal or pituitary problems. Valium is more effective but is addictive and also causes sedation, lethargy, and weight gain, as well as having amnesiac properties and occasionally producing fatal liver failure.

The use of progesterone derivatives and Valium was all that was available to veterinary practitioners in the mid-1980s, however, and the alternative was often the unthinkable. We badly needed a safer and more effective treatment to overcome these difficulties. I am pleased to say that Dr. Lou Shuster and I played a key role in the next development. It all started when I was standing in my garden one day in the spring of 1987 having a conversation with my friend and neighbor, Jim Preston. Jim, a schoolteacher, was explaining to me the horrors of that particular time of his life. His father had just died, he was under a great deal of financial pressure, and his teenage daughter was causing him palpitations with antics such as taking his car without permission and driving it into ditches and walls. It didn't seem like a good time to ask him how things were going, but I did anyway.

"Nick," he said, "I was so stressed out by all the things going on in my life that I couldn't sleep, developed a nervous tic in one eye, and had a really hard time concentrating at school. But I'm OK now—I went to see my doctor and he put me on an anxiety-reducing drug. The medicine made a world of difference to me. Now I sleep like a log, the tic has gone, and I'm back to my old self in the classroom. I feel great. Before this I was in real difficulty. I couldn't function because I couldn't sleep, and I couldn't sleep because I was so worried. Then I started worrying about not sleeping."

"Which medicine did they prescribe?" I asked, fully expecting to be familiar with the class of drug involved, if not the actual name of it.

"Buspirone," he replied. "Have you heard of it?"

Well, I was sorry to admit that I hadn't, but later I found out why it was new to me. Buspirone had been released only one year earlier in human medicine. I went scuttling to my pharmacology tomes, where I learned all I could about the drug and was very impressed with the scientific data backing it up. It was right after this, and following discussions with Lou, that I began prescribing buspirone for a plethora of anxiety-based problems in animals, including, of course, inappropriate elimination in cats. One of the first cases I treated was a nine-year-old spayed female domestic shorthair called Gretchen. Gretchen had been urinating and defecating outside the litter box for almost one year at the time I saw her. I enquired about her medical history and was informed that she had just been to the vet for a medical workup, including urinalysis, but nothing out of the ordinary was found. Gretchen did have a congenital orthopedic problem that caused her to walk peculiarly, but that didn't appear to have anything to do with the elimination problem. At first glance, the litter box arrangements seemed to be adequate, as her owner, a young woman by the name of Pat White, reported what sounded like appropriate positioning of two boxes that both received regular attention.

Gretchen still used the litter box most of the time, and when she did, her behavior in the box sounded pretty normal. So far there were no major clues as to what was going on, but then I asked the sixty-four-thousand-dollar question.

"Where does Gretchen urinate when she doesn't use the box?"

"It's really strange, Dr. Dodman, but most of her indiscretions seem to be targeted at things belonging to me. She usually urinates on my bed, my clothes, or my pocketbook. I've caught her in the act a couple of times. She squats down just like she does in the litter box. Once she urinated right in my face while I was lying in bed."

"What a great compliment," I said, trying to make her feel more comfortable about this revelation. Actually, I had heard this scenario a few times before and the compliment interpretation was only a whisker away from the truth. "What this urination pattern means is that her anxiety is somehow related to you. She is marking you and things that belong to you because she wants to let the world know that you are hers."

Pat's jaw dropped visibly. "So that's what it is," she breathed. "And to think I've been punishing her for it. I suppose punishing her would make her very confused?"

"That's right, especially if the punishment is some time after the event. That will make her even more anxious and more likely to mark," I replied.

We sat in silence for a few moments as I jotted down some notes. Then Pat broke the silence.

"So what do you think she's anxious about?"

"You tell me," I responded. "What changes occurred inside or outside your home one year ago?"

I saw her blush slightly. Then she replied, "Could it have been because my boyfriend, John, moved in with me?"

"That's exactly the sort of change that would cause it. Cats are very much creatures of habit. They like things to stay the same: same house, same routine, same people. Their motto seems to be 'Same is good, change is bad'—fairly simple, really. Any sudden perturbations in the environment, such as construction or people entering or leaving the household, cause them to become insecure. That leads to increased anxiety and marking behavior, including urine marking. Other types of marking may increase, too, for example, butting with the forehead or rubbing against people's legs, but these forms of marking are not distasteful to us, so we don't complain. You can often tell what a cat is anxious about by paying attention to which areas are marked. Marking on a particular person's possessions, or on the person, is a good clue that the anxiety relates to that person. Marking around a window gives a clue that there is something outside that causes the cat concern. Many cats start to urine-mark around windows in the spring, when the screens are put in. The sights, sounds, and odors of the great outdoors, not to mention the increased level of activity of wildlife and various itinerant felines, is often more than a housebound inmate can stand without the need to draw a few lines in the sand."

Pat was intrigued by my explanation and looked as though she could stand to hear more, so I decided to expand a bit more on what I had said. I believe that it helps with treatment to have clients understand as much as possible about behavioral conditions because treatment programs require their intimate cooperation, commitment, and sometimes even inventiveness. I told her about some of the other typical marking sites, including countertops, appliances, heating registers, closets, laundry baskets, desktops, stereo speakers, and anything new, such as shopping bags, cardboard boxes, and even visitors. I did not have a valid explanation for the appliances and heating registers but I hazarded a guess that some physical factors such as warmth or airflow (carrying odors from elsewhere) might just trigger an anxious cat to mark at these sites.

Next I moved on to discuss how Gretchen got on with her new housemate, John. The answer was not encouraging. She would flee from him whenever he came home and would not venture out until he was gone again. She had taken to living almost exclusively in one little-used dining room far from the madding crowd and had essentially become a recluse. I had to do something about that situation, and since the way to a cat's heart is through its stomach, I asked who fed Gretchen. I got the answer I expected: Pat. That would have to change as part of a rehabilitation program designed to endear John to Gretchen. Also, prior to feeding her at night John was to toss out a few food treats for grumpy Gretchen from his armchair by the TV. Following the counterconditioning advice, I moved on to elaborate on the cleanup process, throwing in a few extra tips such as tumble-drying the bedsheets with a lemon-scented dryer sheet. Cats hate citrus and will go a mile to avoid the odor. I first heard this tip from my late grandmother, who insisted that squeezed orange halves on sticks would keep cats out of her vegetable garden. Now there are commercial cat repellents based on the same principle. So much for old wives' tales.

Pat was pleased with the advice but wondered whether there was any medication that would help to make Gretchen feel better immediately. That's when I gave her the lowdown on buspirone and asked if she wanted me to add it to the treatment regimen. The answer was affirmative, so Pat went home to see how she and Gretchen would fare. My first follow-up call with her was one week later, and the news was good. There had not been one single incident of inappropriate urination since the first pill hit the back of Gretchen's throat. Not only that, but she had become extremely outgoing and friendly toward John, who was taking the opportunity to pet her and feed her food treats as though they were going out of fashion. I didn't know it at the time, but increased affection to people is a side effect of buspirone in cats, stemming from their newfound confidence. Some cats also display an increase in kittenish behavior, such as playing with balls of yarn and tearing around the place, but Gretchen wasn't the prototype for this discovery. All in all the treatment was a great success, and the behavioral counterconditioning stood John in good stead when I tapered off the medication a couple of months later.

One of the great things about buspirone is that, unlike with Valium, the learning process is unimpaired, so retraining can proceed at quite a clip. The only glitch with the White case was that Gretchen continued to defecate outside the litter box for a while after the urinary problems were solved. On further questioning, I learned that the location of these accidents was right next to the box in a site more typical of a litter box problem. When I asked Pat to look into this more carefully, she reported that Gretchen appeared to be having problems balancing in the box because of her gimpy legs and had taken to straddling the side of what sounded like a rather small box for her considering her orthopedic problems. I advised a larger box, which eventually took care of this residual problem, but I never did understand why its onset coincided with the anxiety-related urination problem. Undoubtedly there's still more to learn about the cause of these problems.

The buspirone story has burgeoned since the humble beginnings with Gretchen and others. Since then similar success stories have been reported to me time and time again. I was very pleased with the way that buspirone performed in the field and, along with Lou Shuster, took out a U.S. patent to celebrate the fact. Not all cases of what are supposed to be anxiety-related urination behavior respond equally well to treatment, however, and I have begun to wonder whether there isn't a subset of problem urinaters that has some driving force other than anxiety. Studies at the University of California School of Veterinary Medicine indicate that synthetic progesterones, though not as effective as buspirone across the board, do, unlike buspirone, exhibit a differential action between sexes, being much more effective in males. This points to the possibility that undampened male-typical mechanisms may be involved in certain types of inappropriate urination behavior even in neutered cats. This is quite plausible, because masculinization is a process that takes place before birth, and so you would have to intervene extremely early to eliminate all vestiges of maleness. Contrary to popular opinion, castration does not make a male into an "it," only a neutered male whose drive has been tempered by removing the source of testosterone. These thoughts and observations pave the way for future developments in the management of refractory cases and may lead to the next treatment breakthrough.

Another subset of nonresponders may suffer from a newly recognized condition called interstitial cystitis. This condition, which is analogous to a human medical condition bearing the same name, is being diagnosed now because of the advent of fiber-optic cystoscopy. Interstitial cystitis can be confused with bona fide behavioral causes for inappropriate elimination and may have to be ruled out before a behavioral diagnosis can be confirmed, particularly when inappropriate elimination does not respond to conventional therapy. Curiously, a tricyclic antidepressant, Elavil, is recommended for treatment of interstitial cystitis, making one wonder whether anxiety is somehow involved in this condition, too. Psychological factors are known to influence the progression of some illnesses in animals, as evidenced by the irritable bowel syndrome of dogs. Why not an irritable bladder syndrome in cats?

Although it's a lot clearer today than ever before how to deal with a cat that is missing the mark, it is still important to beware of "zebra" diagnoses. When you hear clip-clop-clip outside your window in most cases the sound will be made by a 'horse, but once in a while (rarely), a zebra will be responsible for the sound. Not everything is what it seems at first, so it is always important to keep an open mind. This was emphasized to me by a case I saw a few years back. The case involved a three-year-old neutered male Maine Coon called Harry. During the history-taking part of the session I found that this cat was spraying in the usual range of interesting to bizarre locations. A clear-cut case of anxiety-related urine-marking behavior, I thought, and started to expound to the owners on the possible causes of anxiety in their pet, including the proximity of some prowling neighborhood toms, which I advised should probably be discouraged from their frequent visits. But when I got a good look at Harry as he raised himself from the cat basket I realized there was something I had overlooked. He was massive, a veritable Arnold Schwarzenegger of a cat, with a wide, handsome face and a proud, lionish expression. I had his owners steady him on the examination table while I began to scrutinize him from stem to stern. I felt his head and found that he had thick, mobile plaques of skin on either side of his face, a typical male attribute. He eyed me suspiciously, and I began to have some suspicions about him also. At about this time I became aware of a particularly pungent male smell enveloping him and checked his rear end to make sure he had indeed been castrated. There was nothing to feel. Then I examined his penis to see if it conformed to the normal appearance for a neutered male, that is, small and barbless. That was when my suspicion was confirmed that this allegedly neutered male wasn't neutered at all. His penis could be easily extruded from the sheath and was fully barbed. Harry was in fact a red-blooded male. Further questioning of his owners revealed that he had a serious wanderlust, spending half his life trying to slip outside through partly open doors and picking fights with any other male cats he met. The combination of him smelling like an intact male, looking like an intact male, and behaving like an intact male left me in no doubt that he was not neutered. I don't really know how this comes to be, because a vet who removes only one testicle from a tom must know that there's another one lurking. We can all count to two. Although there exist cats that genuinely have only one testicle (these are called monorchids), this arrangement is as rare as the proverbial hen's tooth. Usually the "missing" testicle is concealed somewhere in the groin or inside the abdomen. This arrangement is referred to as cryptorchidism. Harry was no exception to the usual twofer rule but the story of his incomplete operation had been lost somewhere in the sands of time.

I advised surgery at the earliest convenient time to locate and remove the offending testicle. In Harry's case, I didn't waste time assaying for testosterone to confirm my suspicions because the diagnosis was so clear. Surgery was scheduled for the next week, and on the appointed day I took time out to watch our head of surgery dissect out a small testicle from a fat pad in Harry's groin. The surgery took about five minutes. A few weeks later I saw Harry and his owners back at the hospital for a recheck. He had turned into a perfect angel, just the cat they had always wanted. No spraying and no Houdini moves, and he sure smelled a lot better (and so, I understand, did their house). Not only were the typically male problems gone, but Harry also seemed more relaxed and spent more time with his owners. All in all, it was a satisfactory resolution to the problem. In many ways it's a lot easier to deal with a physical cause for inappropriate elimination behavior than it is to try to resolve nebulous anxiety-based conditions. Unfortunately, though, straightforward medical or surgical solutions are not germane for every Tom, Dick, and Harry.

The next few years should bring even more precise diagnoses of house-soiling problems and yet more effective treatments for the more difficult anxiety-related conditions. Research has accelerated in this area lately and the new information is rapidly finding its way into the field, where it is needed. Hordes of vets are being briefed about these developments, and the revolution has begun. I would like to see widespread adoption of these innovative treatments so that more owners of house-soiling cats can anticipate a satisfactory outcome to these problems. Even with the state of knowledge that exists today, owners need no longer suffer the agonies of having to decide whether to continue to support an old friend who just can't seem to control himself or to opt for the radical alternative of euthanasia. Most of these problems can be solved. All an owner has to do is call the local vet, who should be able to put his or her mind at ease by effectively diagnosing and treating the problem. Finally, it is just a routine veterinary matter.

Eight

The Cat Who Cried
for Help

But it is in the nature of eagles, lions and tigers that they seldom meet with a peaceful end. And this is the essence of the cat as I love it, the inaccessible, unrestrained wild animal.
—KONRAD LORENZ

I never quite know what to expect when I am summoned to the consulting room by one of the other clinicians in our hospital. To some extent, the nature of the inquiry can be predicted from the medical specialty of the clinician requesting assistance. Dermatologists, for example, often solicit an opinion on the likelihood of a psychogenic component to a skin condition, neurologists require input on spinning or seizuring dogs, and exotic-pet specialists sometimes come up with angry iguanas and feather-picking parrots. You can imagine my surprise, then, when one day the call to arms came from a soft-tissue surgeon who was also my department chairman. It was a first. I scurried down the corridors wondering what was in store for me and arrived at the appropriate consulting room in record time. I entered the room cautiously and found my fearless leader, Dr. Tony Schwartz, engrossed in a serious conversation with a rather thin and drawn-looking older woman wearing a battleship gray overcoat. Tony nodded at me and continued to speak with the woman as I slid into the room and took a seat in the gallery. The interlude gave me the opportunity to get a handle on the situation, for everyone knows what they say about putting the brain into gear before engaging the mouth. My immediate assessment when I saw the woman's taut facial expression and fixed stare was that she looked extremely grave and was not buying what Tony was selling. I tuned into the conversation. Suddenly, and to my horror, I realized that she was trying to persuade Tony to devocalize her cat—to remove its vocal cords to prevent it from meowing. Schwartz, in turn, was doing his level best to persuade her that this was not a humane solution to the problem of excessive meowing. I began to understand from what I was hearing that, at this point at least, and from the woman's perspective, there were only two possible solutions to the problem, devocalization or euthanasia. My eyes wandered to beneath the stainless steel examination table, where there was a largish cat carrier, no doubt containing the hapless creature that was the subject of the debate.

A few excruciating minutes later, Tony introduced me to the woman, Ms. Betty Roper, as someone who could probably help her with her problem without recourse to surgery. I was flattered by his confidence but never do enjoy trying to treat behaviors that have such a strong innate component. It's like swimming against the current of nature. Tony began to move toward the door, further endorsing the behavioral solution and issuing various other pleasantries. He then thanked me for my impending involvement, wished Ms. Roper well, and left with a flourish. The room was quiet for a few seconds as Ms. Roper and I positioned ourselves, ready for the next round. Toward the end of the shuffling, friendly, so I decided that if he was still there the next evening I would take him home with me. I took a cat carrier to work the next day just in case. Sure enough, he was still there, and it didn't take much persuading to get him into the carrier. When I got him home, I realized right away that he was an entire male, you know, by the smell, so I made an appointment to have him fixed. The vet said that he thought Thomas was probably about three years old and guessed that he had been owned by someone at one time because he was so friendly toward people. Anyway, shortly after I brought him back to my apartment, I realized that there was another problem. He started sharpening his claws on my furniture and was making a real mess of it. I didn't have time to train him or anything, so I had him declawed. The vet suggested trying a scratching post first, but I didn't have much faith in that idea. The declawing worked out well, but then Thomas started his latest caper, meowing at night. That caused two problems, one for me and one for my neighbors. I couldn't sleep properly because he kept waking me up all night, and my neighbors started to complain because he was disturbing them, too. I tried shutting him out of my bedroom, but he just yowled even louder and I still couldn't get a decent night's sleep. I even tried earplugs, but they didn't help, and I haven't slept properly for weeks. I'm a wreck. Now my landlord is threatening to evict me because the people downstairs keep complaining about the racket, so I don't see that I have any option but to have Thomas demeowed. It's either that or I will have to have him put to sleep, because I know my landlord means business and I have no other place to go."

It sure was a difficult situation for all of us, Thomas included. By the sound of it, Ms. Roper was at the end of her tether, and it wasn't going to be productive to ask her to tolerate his nocturnal vocalizing, even though such behavior is a result of cats' normal crepuscular (dawn and dusk) lifestyle tendencies. In addition, I didn't think she would be overly enthusiastic about engaging in a behavior modification program requiring the investment of her time and attention. As I mused about the possibilities that were open to me, I asked Ms. Roper about Thomas's eating habits and daily activities, with a view to modifying his biological clock. She related what amounted to a day in the life of Thomas, and I found the information quite helpful. Apparently he was fed each morning at seven o'clock, when Ms. Roper was preparing her own breakfast. Following that he would stroll around the apartment while she got ready for work and would often end up in his favorite resting place by a window before she left for work. As Ms. Roper was gone each day from eight until six, she did not know what Thomas did while she was away, but she did notice that when she came home he was usually in his window seat and often going through a stretching and yawning routine. This led Ms. Roper to suspect that he spent much of his day asleep or catnapping. After she was home Thomas would remind Ms. Roper to feed him by crisscrossing in front of her as she walked, apparently trying to trip her up. This behavior, interspersed with a few *rrrrup* noises and leg rubbing, was Thomas's hint that it was mealtime. Ms. Roper was obliged to accommodate this irresistible request for the sake of peace, so Thomas always got his way.

The early evening wasn't much fun for Thomas. His options were to go back to sleep or sit and watch Ms. Roper watching TV. Sometimes she would pet him a little, but he wasn't much of a petting cat even though he was otherwise very friendly. Most nights Ms. Roper went to bed early, leaving his majesty all dressed up with no place to go. This was when the trouble started. Just as the apartment fell silent and the sounds of the night took over, Thomas got his second wind. Whether nighttime reminded Thomas of his days on the run, whether he was answering the call of the wild, or whether he was just crying for help, we anything within reason to save Thomas's neck (or, more precisely, his vocal cords). I saw Ms. Roper raise an eyelid as she gave me a long look.

"OK, I'll try it. But it had better work quickly or I'm going to be out of a home."

I breathed a sigh of relief at this decision and quickly wrote out the prescription before she changed her mind. Using buspirone was a slim chance but a chance nonetheless. At the conclusion of the proceedings I escorted Ms. Roper and Thomas to the front desk to settle up the account.

"I'll give it two weeks," she called back over her shoulder as she reached the doors at the front of the hospital, "but after that I'm not making any promises." And with that she disappeared. I must admit I felt some trepidation at this point, because buspirone can take a few weeks to achieve its effect. However, there was no arguing with the resolute Ms. Roper.

The weeks slipped by after the appointment and Ms. Roper had still not called back. I meant to call her but things kept cropping up. Then one day, when my mind was on something else, I bumped into Tony Schwartz in a corridor.

"Hello, Nick," he said. "I never did thank you properly for the wonderful job you did with Ms. Roper's cat. I know she really appreciated the attention. Thomas did quite well on the medicine, but he still vocalized enough to cause Ms. Roper concern, and she has insisted on the surgery or else she will have him put to sleep."

I had one of those sinking feelings. I was beaten, and Thomas was going to have to pay the price.

A week or so later I heard the news that the surgery had gone well. A hemicordectomy had been performed, which means that only one vocal cord was removed, but the effect is the same, a soft airy noise instead of a real meow. I guessed that Ms. Roper was at last satisfied and out of danger of eviction. Nothing could have been further from the truth. I found this out when she did eventually call me.

"Dr. Dodman," she began, "I know you wanted to avoid Thomas's surgery and so did I, but there was no alternative. He just continued to cry. I want to thank you for all your efforts, but you know, I'm afraid I have to ask for your help one more time. Would you be so kind as to prescribe that medication again for Thomas? It didn't help a lot with the meowing, but it did make him a lot less active at night. Now he is back to running around crazily at night, playing with everything, and he makes so much noise that the neighbors are complaining again. The walls and floors are paper-thin where I live," she added by way of elucidation. "He was much quieter on the medication, and I think he was happier, too."

It was déjà vu. I felt obliged to honor her request or risk Thomas's life. I began to think very hard about the quality of life that Ms. Roper had provided for Thomas. Originally he had been an alley cat without a care in the world except where the next meal was coming from and who would be his date that night. To save him from himself, he had been captured, castrated, declawed, devoiced, and now was to be medicated to make his activity level acceptable to Ms. Roper and her neighbors. I bit the bullet and wrote out another prescription, but I made it clear that this was not a long-term solution and that Ms. Roper should work with Thomas to try to get him to adjust to a new routine, as we had discussed before. She agreed to these terms, and Thomas was remedicated. I know that the results of treatment met with Ms. Roper's approval because as the months went by Ms. Roper asked me for several refills. Finally, she considered Thomas sufficiently well rehabilitated to try tapering off the dose. We both held our breath, but we needn't have. Thomas did just fine.

Maybe he was just more settled, maybe the effects of his neutering had kicked in, or—who knows—maybe Ms. Roper finally got through to him.

It was with some interest that I later read of a similar case of hypervocalization (excessive meowing) in a cat that responded to treatment with the antidepressant Elavil. The case, published in the *Journal of the American Veterinary Medical Association*, reminded me a lot of Thomas's case because the cat in question also failed to respond to behavior modification strategies. Selection of the antidepressant drug Elavil was based on a rationale similar to the one I had employed in Thomas's case. Elavil, like buspirone, has a mood-stabilizing effect, is nonaddictive, and is relatively devoid of sedative side effects. In the published case, the cat started meowing excessively again when the Elavil was withdrawn, so the treatment was reinstated for the long term. I felt that this was a more acceptable solution than surgery. Luckily for cats and vets, Elavil and buspirone are both safe for prolonged use, but an unoperated, medication-free patient is still the ultimate goal. Medications are simply a benign means to an end. I use them when necessary and always with the hope that one day treatment can be withdrawn without disturbing the equilibrium. In explaining this concept to owners I often use the fitting analogy of a magician pulling out a tablecloth from under a tableful of crockery—although I must admit that likening myself to a magician might sound a little egotistical.

A few months after my last communication with Ms. Roper, I was contacted by Gloria, the editor of *Catnip*, a veterinary school publication for cat owners. She requested an interview on the controversial issue of whether to keep cats indoors or allow them freedom to explore the outside environment. As usual, I agreed to help, hoping in some small way to provide enlightenment (or at least food for thought) on an important and controversial issue, and one that I believe has a great influence on our cats' mental health.

"Tell me your feelings about indoor versus outdoor cats," quizzed Gloria. "Are you for letting them go outdoors or against it?"

It was not possible for me to give a simple answer to this question because I knew that there were good reasons to keep cats inside, but then again I had cats like Thomas on my mind. My head told me one thing, but my heart told me another. I decided to sit on the fence of indecision and simply provide the facts.

"It's a lot safer to keep cats indoors," I said somewhat noncommittally. "The average lifespan of an indoor cat is around twelve to fourteen years, while outdoor cats are lucky to reach double digits. I personally have lost three cats prematurely to trauma over the past fifteen years. Two were struck by vehicles on a fairly quiet road in front of my first house, and the other was killed by a roaming neighborhood dog."

As I spoke I recollected the sad scene at one of these accidents. Vicky, my daughter by a previous marriage, who was then three years old, found her cat, Daisy, lying dead at the side of the road. When I got there she looked up into my face and said, "Daddy, will you please take my cat to the hospital and make her well again?" I had to swallow hard before giving her an early lesson about the finality of death.

Because of experiences like this I have certainly had cause to think long and hard about letting future cats out. At present, partly because of my wife's strong feeling that our cats should remain indoors where they're safest, I have reluctantly agreed to deny Cinder and Monkey the pleasure of outdoor life—not that that stops them from bursting out at every opportunity.

"If safety and longevity were the only considerations," I continued with Gloria, "the answer to the indoor/outdoor question would be simple: keep cats in."

"Are there any other dangers besides trauma associated with the outdoor lifestyle?" Gloria probed.

"You bet. It's a veritable jungle out there. Infected bites from other cats leading to the development of abscesses are epidemic in the outdoor cat population. When I was a new graduate, an experienced veterinary practitioner once said to me that if I was consulted about a cat with an unexplained fever, nine times out of ten the problem would be an abscess, and I have found that to be true. Cats will be cats, and fighting over territory or mates is one of the things that they do for a living, especially if they're not neutered. There are other, even more serious infections that may occur in unvaccinated outdoor cats, including rabies and feline leukemia. These conditions are passed on by bite wounds. The word about the dangers of outdoor living must be out, because about half of America's sixty million cats are currently living indoors. Many owners appear to be concluding that the safety of indoor life outweighs any problems it may cause."

"Do I detect some reticence in your present conclusions, Dr. Dodman?" the editor asked perspicaciously. "Could it be that you don't think indoor life is all that it's cracked up to be?"

"How very observant of you," I said, finally getting off the fence of noncommitment. "I have always had concerns about restricting cats' freedom because it seems so unnatural to confine any creature with a free spirit. I realize that my feelings are countered by the existing empirical evidence against giving cats their freedom, but I see many cats stressed as a result of confinement."

"Please explain," Gloria said patiently.

"In nature, cats have an extensive home range, the area over which they roam. Even one square mile is not an unusually large area for them to frequent. They spend a good deal of their active time patrolling this area, exploring, hunting, and breeding, and will actively defend a portion of it, which we term their territory. If you take this interest away from them, all they have left is survival. The situation reminds me of Chief Seattle's famous speech as he signed over his tribe's lands to the white man, cautioning that destruction of the buffalo, the forests, and the land would lead to an existence of mere survival instead of one in which people take joy in living. I sometimes wonder whether we aren't guilty of creating a similar situation for our pets when we incarcerate them. It's safer, yes, but at what cost? I see a lot of behavior problems that I feel sure are the products of confinement and a relatively purposeless life. Behaviors such as vocalization and urine marking can be intensified and performed inappropriately in cats confined inside the house. I also see completely abnormal behaviors, such as compulsive wool sucking, self-licking, and self-mutilation. Some of the behaviors I encounter are uncommon or even unheard-of in feral cats, but such behavior problems are ubiquitous in the indoor cat population. The incidence of these problems is much lower in cats in Britain, where most are indoor/outdoor cats that are allowed to come and go at will. In all likelihood, many of the behavior problems we see in cats in the United States are a direct result of confinement and an unnatural lifestyle. The cartoonist Gary Larson depicted cat stress in his own inimitable way when he drew a cat pressed firmly against a window observing an accident between two vehicles outside. The accident involved a pair of trucks that had collided, spewing their contents all over the street. One truck contained 'Al's Small Flightless Birds' and the other 'Bill's Performing Rodents.' The result was what a behaviorist might refer to as an unresolvable dilemma for the cat—a humorous interpretation of the type of real-life conflict that indoor living facilitates.

"Some people may disagree, saying that outside life is stressful, too, and a darn sight more dangerous. In a way they're right, and in a way they're not. Indoor life is associated with more behavior problems, and behavior problems are the leading cause of death in cats because frustrated owners (too often) surrender their cats for euthanasia. Outdoor life is, as my late father would have said, a short but merry one. If a cat is to be allowed outside, it should be neutered and fully vaccinated first. It should also be allowed out only in a safe environment, away from busy roads, and only during the day to prevent encounters with various forms of nocturnal wildlife. Owning an indoor/outdoor cat, what I call the British solution, may be something of a compromise, but I see it as the nearest thing to achieving the best of both worlds."

Gloria thanked me for my contribution, and our conversation drew to a close. I read a rough draft of the article a couple of weeks later and thought that it was OK, although a lot of my hedging and provisos about life outside had been cut out. *C'est la vie*, I thought. But as it turned out, I should have been a little more insistent. A while later I received a letter from California. What follows is the letter (verbatim) so that you can see how high feelings run on this matter.

Friday, July 28, 1995

Dr. Dodman:

While my beloved cats were alive, I had a subscription to your CATNIP. I chanced upon #10, Vol. 2 January 1995 copy and reread it.

I noted Page 3's THE INDOOR LIFE and the paragraph "From the cat's point of view, 'life outside is a short but merry one.' "

I wonder how far up your *** your head is that prevents your blindness in seeing that an outdoor—particularly a stray outdoor cat's life—is not only not merry, but is down right, dammed right ugly and filled with suffering and more than occasionally, excruciatingly painful.

I feed strays and a friend and I trap them when possible. A vet's exam reveals whether they can be neutered and homes found or if they must be put to sleep. We've found them with hunks of flesh torn from their necks, with tumors that have caused them to burst. We've found them with such horrendous respiratory illness nothing could save their lives. We've found them starving, tails cut off, eyes poked out, hog-tied and beaten.

This is a merry life?

Either you're living in a dream world or you're so insane you should be put away before you endanger any living things.

Get a grip on reality (or are you a member of the Church of Religious Science, to whose members, no matter how horrible things are, everything is just perfect?)

You get the advanced head up the *** of the month award, plus the jerk of the month and the air head moron of the month awards. Congratulations. If you are unable to read this, perhaps one of your merry stray cats will do so for you.

Idiot.

I realized right away that this lady was no fan of mine. (What's more, she didn't appear to be a lady according to the definition of the word.) She obviously disagreed violently with what I had said, but I thought she had missed the point. Despite her tone and scary gift for the vernacular, I felt obliged to reply. I thought I should remain relatively civil because without that composure I would never score a point—and besides, she had my address and I had only her post office box number.

August 15, 1995

Dear Ms. Scott,

There are about 60 million cats in the U.S. Twenty percent of this population is put to sleep annually in shelters or in veterinary offices. One half of the mortality is accounted for by "behavior problems" which plague, in particular, the indoor cat.

This is the single biggest cause of feline mortality and my mission is to do what I can to minimize it. I realize that being a stray can be a dangerous and miserable life and I was not suggesting that all cats should simply be turned "free." My comments were intended for domestic cat owners who have a choice of an indoor cat or an indoor/outdoor cat. The latter by the way is the norm in Britain and most of the British cats are well and happy. Also, British cats are not plagued by the same psychoses that keep U.S. behaviorists busy. Nevertheless I did not intend for people to make indoor/outdoor cats out of their pets without serious thought. As I stated in my interview, the life expectancy of an indoor/outdoor cat is reduced by trauma and disease (but not tumors). An owner would have to select where and when to permit freedom—not, for example, next to a busy road. The fact that cats prefer to roam is undeniable. The fact that it is dangerous (like life outside prison) is a given. I have always agonized about whether to permit freedom and danger or to insist on confinement and, in some cases, the obvious psychological pressures which result.

You and I have the same mission, to help cats, but we work at different ends of the spectrum. You see the worst that can happen to the permanently lost cat. I see the worst that can happen to the permanently interred cat. My expression "short life and a merry one" was not meant to mean that outdoor cats are merry. The expression (which may not be interpreted this way by Americans) really refers to a Faustus-like situation—one of "live now, pay later." They want to go outside but it is dangerous and may lead to loss of health or life. I keep my cats in all the time (unless they escape) and have to live with their languishing looks and slightly neurotic indoor cat behavior. It's hard to know what is right but, for the time, I have settled for the "Hotel California" situation.

By the way, indoor cats also get many disgusting diseases

(including fatal respiratory infections, which sometimes sweep homes or catteries). Some are overfed and obese, hardly able to move, some take to biting their tails in frustration (and have to have them amputated), and some are declawed (have their fingers cut off) for scratching furniture (a normal behavior leading to the most painful surgery of all). It's not all roses inside the home either.

Have a nice day.
Nicholas H. Dodman

I never heard back from this angry woman and have always wondered what her response was to reading my letter. Did she just give up on me as a lost cause, not believing a word I said? Did she get even angrier and start sticking pins in an effigy of me? Or did she suddenly realize that we were both trying to help cats in our own ways and that there had been some kind of misunderstanding? In retrospect, we were both talking about a different population of cats. I feel almost certain that her experiences were with feral cats—cats that live and breed in the wild and do not belong to anyone. I realize that pet cats can get lost and become absorbed into this population but do not believe this is common when a cat is fed and looked after in one location by a family that cares and spends time at home.

So what does all this indoor/outdoor cat stuff have to do with Thomas and his excessive vocalization? Quite a lot, I would say, but it still wouldn't have helped us reach a satisfactory conclusion about what to do with him. If he had been left out, he would probably have died before too long, but not before fathering many unwanted kittens to follow in his paw prints. Ms. Roper could never have let him out, either, because she lived near a main road, and anyway he would never have come back. Perhaps she should have considered placing him in another home, but for some reason that was not an option for her. Another possibility would have been to free him in some safe area after neutering and vaccinating him. Even this "irresponsible" solution might have been better for him than what did eventually befall him at the hands of this Samaritan.

My wife and I did one of these capture-and-release moves a few years back with a neighborhood stray that adopted us and kept visiting us at the back door. We didn't feel we could take him into our already crowded home, but we did want to help him, so one day we apprehended him, vaccinated and neutered him, gave him a square meal, and set him free. It seems he must have enjoyed the experience because he wouldn't leave us alone after that. We eventually solved the dilemma by buying him an airline ticket to Washington, D.C., where he now lives happily with my father-in-law, Ted. Oh, and by the way, he goes out whenever he wants to and never gets into any trouble that he doesn't want to. Wolfey, as we call him, has street smarts and will probably live to a ripe old age, even at large in the D.C. suburbs. He is a Top Cat kind of cat, a true survivor and leader of the gang—and he's healthy (if not slightly overweight), wealthy (in terms of the affection he receives), and happy.

So now everyone is totally confused. "For crying out loud," I hear you say, "what on earth do I do? Should I choose incarceration and safety for my cat, or freedom and risk? Thomas's existence or Wolfey's?" I can say only that the final decision on how to deal with the young and the restless remains with the individual and depends to a great extent on the personality and experience of the cat and the circumstances in which the owners find themselves. I have ended up with the indoor option for my cats, and for the most part they seem to have come to grips with it. Anyway, I'm sure they could not fend for themselves in the big wide world now. If I lived in the country and was starting over again with a couple of kittens, I would have to rethink the whole matter. Perhaps if they kept me awake all night by caterwauling it would help me to reach a decision more rapidly.

Back to Konrad Lorenz again—for the last line this time—as he obviously gave the matter some thought. He summarized the situation as follows: "It is certainly not my intention to dissuade anyone from keeping a cat in a town flat. The town dweller has few enough contacts with nature, and a handsome unspoilt cat may well bring a touch of it into a city street, but I maintain that one can only appreciate the full charm of its being by giving a cat its freedom. . . . One can win not the apparent but the real love of a cat in no greater measure than by allowing it its natural way of living, and by seeking tactfully to approach it in its own natural surroundings. At the same time, one must accept the fact that the animal whose inmost wishes one thus respects is exposed to all the dangers that normally threaten such a small beast of prey. . . . None of my own cats died a natural death."

Nine

The Rebel Without Claws

For several weeks my wife, Linda, had been asking me to talk with one of her clients, Holly Hines, who was apparently having terrible trouble with her cat, McTavish. McTavish was mutilating highly visible parts of Holly's favorite furniture by indulging in his favorite pastime of sharpening his claws. Linda had invested many hours trying to talk Holly out of declawing McTavish and had explained all the alternatives as clearly and emphatically as she could. Holly remained noncommittal. To Holly, declawing seemed the best solution because it was guaranteed to solve the problem. A few quick snips of his front claws under anesthesia, she thought, and McTavish would never vandalize furniture again. She was desperate for a solution and probably wasn't listening too well as Linda tried to explain the downside of the procedure.

The message Holly was supposed to receive was that declawing involves more than simply trimming a cat's nails to the quick; it actually involves amputation of the tips of the digits, bones and

all. The inhumanity of the procedure is clearly demonstrated by
the nature of cats' recovery from anesthesia following the surgery.
Unlike routine recoveries, including recovery from neutering surgeries, which are fairly peaceful, declawing surgery results in cats
bouncing off the walls of the recovery cage because of excruciating pain. Cats that are more stoic huddle in the corner of the
recovery cage, immobilized in a state of helplessness, presumably
by the overwhelming pain. Declawing fits the dictionary definition of mutilation to a tee. Words such as *deform, disfigure, disjoint,*
and *dismember* all apply to this surgery. Partial digital amputation
is so horrible that it has been employed for torture of prisoners of
war, and in veterinary medicine, the clinical procedure serves as a
model of severe pain for testing the efficacy of analgesic drugs.
Even though analgesic drugs can be used postoperatively, they
rarely are, and their effects are incomplete and transient anyway,
so sooner or later the pain will emerge. However quickly cats
forget the hideous experience of declawing, and even though
they may not hold grudges, that doesn't seem sufficient justifica-
tion for putting a family pet through such a repugnant experience.
It was this kind of information that Linda shared with Holly in
the hope that she would entertain the idea of behavior modification instead of the deplorable surgical alternative.

In attempting to persuade Holly to try behavior modification
therapy, Linda also explained the disadvantages facing declawed
cats in the wild, especially regarding self-defense and shinning up
trees to escape danger. There has been a recent survey that
seems to indicate that declawing does not impair cats' ability to
fend for themselves in the wild, but this finding is counterintui-
tive and difficult to believe. The relevance of a study is determined by its methodology, and if I recall correctly, this study
relied on owner opinion rather than hard data, so the results
should be taken with a grain of salt. Anyway, how well McTavish

could look after himself outside was not a major factor in his case, as he rarely got out.

Despite Linda's best attempts to encourage Holly to adopt a conservative approach, Holly was hesitant to commit to a behavior modification program and still leaned toward the more expedient surgical solution. It was with this backdrop that I called Holly to arrange for a behavioral consultation (gratis) to discuss ways to deter or redirect young McTavish from his annoying pastime. I must admit I didn't get around to making the call immediately because I had a lot going on at work, but I did eventually get around to it. I didn't talk with Holly directly but left messages on her answering machine at home and at work. At least the ball was now in her court. I arrived home later the same evening to find Linda staring blankly at her computer screen. As I approached she looked up with a stunned expression. She informed me that she had just heard back from Holly Hines and that the news was not what we wanted to hear. Apparently I was a day late and a dollar short because Holly had taken McTavish to another vet a couple of weeks earlier and the deed had already been done. Holly had added, for good measure, that she and McTavish had no regrets and that they were both better off for her decision. Who was she kidding? My wife felt let down and was angry with herself for not appreciating the urgency of the situation. That evening she spent many hours going over what she could have done to alter the outcome, but it was water under the bridge.

Feelings run strong on declawing, and there are several different camps. There are those people who have their cats declawed without so much as a second thought. These are the same people who believe that it is quite painless to castrate a camel by crushing its testicles between two rocks—unless you get your fingers caught between the rocks. Sadly, some vets fall into this category and offer declawing as part of the well-kitten package along with vaccination and deworming. At the other end of the spectrum are people who would like to see the procedure banned. There are, of course, many positions between these extremes, but to my mind the most reasonable one is that of attempting to avoid the procedure at any cost—except when the alternative is euthanasia. Linda and I both fight to avoid declawing, which can be a pain for some of our clients, but not for the patients.

You can imagine how I felt in my lecture course when a guest lecturer stood up and advocated surgery as a viable treatment for furniture clawing. This lecturer, who moments before had proudly announced how infrequently she needed to use behavior-modifying drugs, elaborated on how effective declawing was in her own cats. I didn't want to leave the veterinary students with the impression that declawing was the way to curb furniture clawing and felt obliged to tell the other side of the story. With some trepidation I rose to my feet and attempted a polite rebuttal. However, tact and diplomacy are not my strong suit and what I had to say was diametrically opposed to what had already been said, so in a way it was a given that my comments would be regarded as contentious.

"Dr. Wilson," I said, "has just informed us about how little she employs drug treatment to assist in the management of behavior problems. I don't know why anyone would want to make such a claim because drugs, when used correctly, relieve pain and suffering and can expedite recovery. At the veterinary schools in California and Pennsylvania, and at our own veterinary school, pharmacologic supportive therapy is used in thirty to seventy percent of behavioral cases now, and to good effect. Cat cases would be included in the upper end of this percentage range because the problems they present are less amenable to behavior modification than those of dogs. Purposely avoiding the use of drugs, especially when dealing with cat problems, seems more of an omission than a recommendable strategy and I don't see any sense in it. Painful surgical solutions to behavioral problems, however, are a different matter and should not be undertaken lightly, if at all."

That did it. Dr. Wilson reiterated her position and proceeded to further denigrate the use of drugs. Having this conflict in front of the students was not appreciated by them; it's difficult enough being a student without having your teachers disagree and contradict each other over the subject matter of the course. Under normal circumstances I would have waited until later to voice my opinion, but after years in the anesthesia trenches watching the painful recoveries of the victims of this surgery, I couldn't let the situation pass without immediate comment. The complaints about our public disagreement poured in, and the conflict between the two of us continued behind the scenes. Even today we enjoy only a brittle peace during our now limited professional encounters. It's a case of once bitten (or scratched), twice shy for both of us.

Perhaps my views on what I consider mutilations stem from my British heritage. On the other side of the pond we are particularly concerned about animal welfare and have banned many of the cosmetic and convenience surgeries on animals that are routine in the United States. One highly regarded British textbook by Turner and Bateson on the biology of cat behavior concludes a short section on scratching behavior with the following statement: "The operative removal of the claws, as is sometimes practiced to protect furniture and curtains, is an act of abuse and should be forbidden by law in all, not just a few countries." That just about sums it up for me, too. But if you make the moral decision to join the ranks of the claw conservatives, what do you do when your cat starts tearing up your furniture? Are there things you can do to circumvent the problem, or do you just have to lock your furniture away behind closed doors? The answers are yes, there are, and no, you don't have to, but to make inroads on this thorny problem, it helps to understand the motivation of the behavior.

The simple explanation that furniture clawing is primarily conducted to sharpen the claws just doesn't work for me. To use an analogy, why would dragging a bunch of fishhooks across an armchair do anything to improve the sharpness of their barbs? Furniture clawing does not *sharpen* the claws; it conditions them by exercising muscles and helping to shuck off dead nail husks (which may be found on the ground beneath a well-used scratching site). Another reason why cats stretch up and sink their claws into furniture is that it feels good. We all enjoy a good stretch, especially after a nap. But the story doesn't end there. Scratching and clawing at various objects is also a form of visual and olfactory marking behavior. The visual marking aspect is easy to appreciate. The mark says, "Kilroy was here." Remember at school when all the property was inscribed with hieroglyphics such as "This desk belongs to John Smith"? It's the same principle. Because of this, claw marks are always strategically positioned in a highly visible location, such as the arm of a couch facing the door (not the one facing the wall). One of my colleagues has a photograph of a well-scratched tree on someone's front lawn. The tree stands alone, right in the middle of the lawn. There are plenty of trees all around the property, but one neighborhood cat has chosen this sore thumb of a tree as the object on which to underscore its presence. Typical for a cat.

The olfactory component of scratching adds a more subtle component to this marking behavior. Scent marking to a cat is like writing to a person, conveying a message long after the sender has gone. Pheromonal odors released from scent glands in the paws leave no doubt in another feline mind as to exactly who

Kilroy was and probably what he was thinking when he last passed by. It's as if the visual cue were a signpost directing attention to the more detailed message. This is one explanation of why declawed cats continue to go through the motions of furniture scratching when they have no claws to sharpen and no visible fruits of their labor. Another explanation for the vacuous scratching of such cats is that they are ritualistically acting out behavior that is hardwired into their neural circuits. In other words, they keep doing it even when there is no apparent reason to do so, because they feel compelled.

As scratching has a marking function, and marking is intensified by stress, the frequency of scratching should increase as tensions build, and this does indeed appear to be the case. In one situation I encountered, a resident cat began to scratch the edge of an open door to the living room when a new cat was introduced to the home. This territorial response mirrors what happens with urine marking, too. Taking things a little further, it should be possible for a naturalistic behavior such as scratching to be expressed compulsively. The result would be excessive and apparently pointless furniture scratching, and careful examination of the situation might reveal a sensitive individual under stress. Theoretically, the tendency to respond to stress in this way would run in families, and furniture clawing appears to do just that. It is common knowledge that to avoid owning a compulsive scratcher, you should select a kitten from parents who do not indulge in this behavior to excess. Care should be exercised in interpreting this as evidence of a genetic tendency for anxiety, however, as learning is known to be involved when it comes to scratching. A careful analysis would have to be made before definitive conclusions could be drawn about the various contributions of nature and nurture, of temperament and learning, to the transmission of this behavior from one generation to another. It would be an interesting study and one that would point the way forward. Treatment of compulsive scratch marking (if that's what it is) would involve minimizing environmental stress such as intercat conflict, redirecting the scratching onto an acceptable target, and perhaps in refractory cases the judicious use of anxiety-reducing medication. This strategy reflects the influence of treatments developed for another form of compulsive marking behavior, compulsive urine marking.

Let's suppose for a moment that we are dealing not with a compulsive cat but simply with one that periodically blows off steam by shredding a couple of high-profile chairs around the house. This is not a cat for the obsessive-compulsive disorder clinic, but merely one who needs to have its energies channeled along more acceptable lines. This is where the scratching post comes in, and scratching posts *do* work if you know something about how to choose them and where to place them. The best teacher of the noble art of scratching is the cat's own mother, but if she isn't around or isn't trained to use a scratching post, that leaves it all up to us. The first rule is that scratching posts should be tall enough for the cat to stretch up full length and arch its back as it sinks its claws in. Also, at least one post should be positioned close to your cat's normal resting area. It's typical for a cat to want to have a good clawing stretch after a decent sleep. The second rule is that scratching posts should be absolutely secure. Cats think there's nothing worse than having the post wobble or fall over when they're in the middle of a good stretch. Third, the post has to be covered with the right kind of stuff. Tightly wrapped, uninteresting carpet is out, and burlap and other easily shreddable things are in. Cats prefer vertically oriented fibers, as this orientation lends itself to shredding. Many owners change a scratching post when it is old and tattered. This is dead wrong, as shredding indicates frequent use and that is exactly what you want. Half the fun cats experience from a scratching post derives from getting their claws stuck in the material and leaving wispy threads as testimony of their erstwhile presence. More than one post is usually preferred, perhaps one for each high-traffic area of the house. Different kinds of scratching posts will provide different challenges, so owners can profitably get quite creative. A large log (with bark) is apparently lots of fun and especially good for those conditioning functions. Scratching posts should start out in front of previously scratch-marked locations or at least in high-profile sites. It may be awkward for the humans to have to circumnavigate an assortment of burlap-wrapped posts in the center of living areas, especially at night when the lights are out, but fear not, these obstacles can be inched to more-convenient locations over time.

Sometimes a reluctant cat can be persuaded to start using a scratching post by trickery. One of the tricks is to lace with catnip the fabric bound to the post. It has been estimated that only a third of cats experience the seductive effects of catnip (for the others, alternative olfactory attractions could be devised), but the reason for this discrepancy remains obscure. Partakers roll around in apparent ecstasy, salivating and looking for all the world like a female in heat. Some people believe that the response to catnip is sexual, but there are several strikes against this proposal. A compelling one is that catnip elicits the same heatlike behavior in both males and females. However, we now know sexual behaviors are not exclusive for one sex or the other, just more likely in a particular sex, so one cannot absolutely rule out this theory. It has also been suggested that catnip evokes a predatory response, but that interpretation has been challenged because there are responses shown by cats under the influence of catnip that are not part of the cat's normal predatory behavioral repertoire. It would seem counterproductive, for example, for a cat to salivate its way toward an unsuspecting prey, pausing occasionally to roll on its back and wriggle around on the ground. The prospective lunch may die laughing, but that would be the cat's only hope. Whatever the correct explanation for the effects of catnip, it appears to be a lot of fun for cats and may even attract them to a desired location, such as a scratching post, for instance.

While attracting your cat to the desired location for its scratching, it is important simultaneously to deter the scratching of inappropriate sites, such as your stereo speakers or the arm of your favorite chair. To do this you can take advantage of the cat's normal aversion to aluminum foil or plastic wrap by applying either material around target areas. For difficult-to-wrap locations, aversive odors, such as citrus-scented sprays, can be applied, often to good effect. The French behaviorist Dr. Pageat believes that pheromone-containing oily secretions from the glands between the cat's eyes and ears serve as an olfactory deterrent to scratching. The message sent is "Already claimed—paws off." Using an opposite strategy, I have often contemplated using commercial odor neutralizers to invalidate the message but so far have only got around to using citrus-scented odor maskers (OK, so I used lemon-scented furniture polish and ruined the furniture anyway).

If all of the above fails, there is a relatively new solution to furniture scratching that I know works in some cases at least. I refer to the use of Soft Paws. These soft plastic caps are simply glued onto the cat's claws, rendering them less pointy and less likely to damage fabric. I have clients who are jubilant about the success they have had with these faux nails. They come in several colors, too, so your cat can sport a selection of fashionable colors while still being able to enjoy a good, well-anchored stretch and some undetectable scent-marking behavior. Soft Paws can be quite a surprise for an unsuspecting veterinarian. The first time I

saw a cat with blue nails it threw me for a loop until I realized
what was going on. At first I thought the owner might have a
toenail-painting fetish, but no, the truth was much less interesting.

By one means or another, armed with the correct information,
we humans should be able to redirect or otherwise contain a
furniture-scratching feline. However, cats are formidable strate-
gists, and sometimes it can be quite a challenge to contain their
behavior. One owner, responding to an article on furniture
scratching in our feline publication, *Catnip*, reported yet another
reason cats scratch. With regard to her eleven-year-old male cat,
Smokey, she wrote:

*I have a "scratcher" who defies the norms outlined in your
[magazine]. He is an indoor/outdoor cat who is allowed out all
day when it is fine, but I keep him in at night (he objects to this
and sometimes fights to get out but I'm bigger so I win!). I have
several trees on the property and I notice that he uses all of them
for scratching and climbing purposes. However, he is also an
indoor scratcher, but not for any of the reasons outlined in your
article. He scratches the back of the sofa for my attention when he
wants to go out. He didn't always do this. He used to sit and
stare at me for a while—cats are very good at this. When this
didn't work he would become vocal, displaying an interesting
range of meows, yips, and yelps. If I was so inclined I would
then get up and let him out. When I wasn't responding fast
enough to suit him, however, he would sashay across the floor to
the back of the sofa, looking at me all the while (I caught this
action with my peripheral vision), and start to give it a good
going-over with his claws. This, as you might expect, got my
attention fast, and he got what he wanted. He succeeded in
ruining two slipcovers by tearing them completely to shreds. He*

still pulls this stunt but, by a stroke of good fortune, I have minimized the damage he inflicts. I recently purchased a new sofa, not because of the cat but because I liked the sofa. The covering is a hard burlap-type of densely woven material and his nibs gets nowhere with it. Despite the scratching, the covering remains intact. Lucky me, I could easily have chosen damask or some other easily tearable material.

I don't think a scratching post would have worked with this dude. He has the kind of personality that leads him to do the unconventional. He is a nonconformist, as I am. We make a good team.

Reason number four why cats scratch furniture excessively: The behavior can be reinforced by conditioning. Getting attention for engaging in a behavior will usually increase the frequency of that behavior. This woman's story about Smokey illustrates the point that dealing with behavior problems involves more than simply applying a set of empirical rules to treat the problem at hand. A detailed account of the behavior is needed to establish where and when it occurs, and what precedes and what follows the cat's actions. Only with such attention to fine detail can effective behavior modification programs be designed. Smokey's owner was right in that he probably wouldn't have used a scratching post—he wasn't scratching the furniture for the usual catty reasons. He had learned that this (bad) behavior got him what he wanted, and as unconventional as he may have been in other respects, he was conforming well to the tenets of operant conditioning. Although his owner was satisfied with her fortuitous "indestructible sofa" solution, another strategy that would have worked (eventually) in this case would have been to ignore the sofa scratching and train Smokey to another cue. At least Smokey's owner didn't opt for the surgical solution for her rebel.

She found her own way around the problem—and there are many imaginative and conventional solutions that can be tried before resorting to the travesty of amputation. To update an old saying, there's more than one way to cure a cat.

Ten

In the Heat of
the Night

Tara Woods had always wanted a kitten, but her parents wouldn't let her have one, and neither would the landlord of their three-decker apartment in Worcester. Finally, when she was twenty-three, she moved into her own place and realized her life-long dream, acquiring what she believed to be the cutest kitten in the city. Tara's new arrival, named Pebbles, came from a friend whose own cat had unexpectedly produced a litter the summer before. From an outsider's perspective Pebbles was not all that remarkable; she was young (six months old, to be precise), a domestic shorthair cat (aren't they all?), and jet black. Her redeeming features were that she had great personality, was as cute as a button, and was loved.

Everything was going according to plan. Tara was as pleased as a cat with two tails and was having fun playing with Pebbles at every possible opportunity. Pebbles responded by returning the affection several times over, and kitten and owner became really close. It was an ideal arrangement—until one day Pebbles's behavior was totally different. From an affectionate, loving cat she became a discontented soul in what seemed like a Jekyll-and-Hyde metamorphosis. She just wouldn't settle down and paced back and forth in the apartment crying, occasionally stopping at a window to gaze out longingly. Pebbles would still stop and rub against Tara's leg once in a while, but her attentions were fleeting, and within seconds she would resume the relentless pacing immediately, as if she had some hidden agenda. In the middle of this activity Pebbles would sometimes crouch low on the ground and arch her back, moaning and clawing at the carpet. Then she would roll and squirm, contorting her body into all sorts of weird positions as if in pain. She also started to spend much more time around the litter box, although the results of her constant efforts to urinate were underwhelming.

Tara was completely confused by this behavior. What was going on? She knew something was wrong but had no idea what. Frustrated, Tara called the friend she had gotten Pebbles from to get a second opinion. The two of them discussed the possibilities of poisoning, a urinary tract infection, and even seizures before deciding that they were stumped for an answer and needed expert help. Tara called the veterinary school late that Sunday night, hoping for some advice. I wasn't on call, but a colleague, Dr. Nishi Dhupa, took the call and told her to come in right away so that she could examine Pebbles.

Relieved, Tara hopped into her car and raced to the clinic, Pebbles beside her in a cat carrier. As if to confirm the urgency of the situation, Pebbles cried the whole way. It was not her usual cry, but rather a baleful, drawn-out, hollow-sounding cry from the heart. Tara drove faster.

When she arrived at the clinic Dr. Dhupa escorted her to the examination room.

"Please tell me again about the signs that Pebbles is showing,"

Dr. Dhupa asked as she opened the carrier, allowing Pebbles to slink around the floor.

Tara went through her story once more, recounting Pebbles's writhing and moaning as Dr. Dhupa observed Pebbles carefully.

Dr. Dhupa said nothing but lifted Pebbles onto the stainless steel exam table and began her physical examination of the cat. Occasionally she paused to scribble something on the record. It was a tense moment for Tara.

Finally Dr. Dhupa put her pen down and looked up, smiling.

"You have nothing to worry about, Ms. Woods. Pebbles is in good health and the behavior you have been witnessing is normal. You see, Pebbles is in heat."

Tara's jaw dropped. She was both relieved and surprised. It hadn't occurred to her that such a young cat could suddenly, in the middle of winter, feel the urge to mate. Even if she had expected Pebbles to go into heat that early, she would never have recognized the signs for what they were because she had never seen a cat in heat before. None of her friends' cats had ever been in heat while she was around, and she had no idea the behavioral change was so dramatic. Who would have thought that a cat would make so much fuss about it? All that moaning, squirming, rolling, clawing, and urinating was normal and part of the game. Suddenly Tara's relief turned to embarrassment as she realized her mistake, but Dr. Dhupa consoled her by mentioning a number of conditions that could cause similar signs. The list featured various neurological problems, including rabies and distemper, and any one of a number of toxins and metabolic problems. Tara felt less silly after hearing that and bundled Pebbles into the carrier for the ride home.

"I knew what was going on the moment I took her temperature," Dr. Dhupa said to Tara as she was leaving. "When I put the thermometer into her rectum she thrust her rump in the air and splayed her legs. That posture is a characteristic response of cats in heat."

The two women smiled at each other and parted company, Tara clutching discharge orders. Needless to say, the orders contained strict instructions to get Pebbles spayed at the earliest opportunity following the heat period.

Even if you know what to expect, estrus (or heat) behavior in a female cat is pretty tough to tolerate. Not only that, but if all the extroverted behavior succeeds in its intended goal of attracting the opposite sex, you can receive numerous unwelcome visits from cruising neighborhood toms, whose noisy outdoor presence simply adds to the confusion. Another unpleasant aspect of having the toms hanging around is that they advertise their presence by urinating on your shrubs, your doorstep, and your windows. This doesn't ride well with most folks, who open their doors and windows on a beautiful spring day only to be suffocated by an odor of tomcat urine so thick you could cut it with a knife. These drawbacks, plus nocturnal battles between suitors, are usually enough reason to send even long-suffering owners running for help. It's not as if heat occurs once or twice a year, either, because cats are seasonally polyestrus, which means that they are the reproductive equivalents of the Energizer bunny and just keep cycling throughout the long breeding season, from January until October. What's more, cats are in heat for about nine of the twenty-one days of their cycle unless they are bred (or otherwise fooled into thinking they've been bred). The reason why mating shortens the heat period is that cats are induced ovulators, that is, they release their eggs as a result of the physical act of mating, and following this the heat subsides.

Spaying females is definitely the way to go if you do not intend to breed your cat. It prevents unwanted estrus behavior and, as a bonus, probably reduces the incidence of mammary cancer later in life. Mammary cancer is not uncommon in older cats, and when it occurs it is usually malignant, so neutering is a smart move for that reason alone. The major reason for neutering cats, however, is birth control. Unwanted kittens—and most kittens not born of a deliberate breeding turn out to be unwanted—simply add to the already staggering mortality figures as they find their way to the nation's shelters and pounds. Alternatively, they end up homeless and roaming around, a liability and a hazard to themselves and others.

To digress for a moment, there are about sixty million owned cats in the United States, but there are also forty million unowned cats who have to try to fend for themselves in the wild. Some of these ownerless cats were originally raised in homes and are reasonably well socialized. Others, a few generations down the line, are unsocialized and feral. Even the first group of ownerless but previously socialized cats is worrisome enough, as they do not fare well in the wild, lacking the skills to survive in the urban jungle. As a result they end up suffering all kinds of inhumanities and are constantly exposed to the threats of trauma and disease. In addition, they remain unvaccinated and, from the public health point of view, could be construed as a health hazard, serving as a bridge between rabid wild animals and the human population. True feral cats also pose a problem. Even though they are more adept at survival than previously owned cats and are less likely to approach humans, they can't be allowed to reproduce unchecked, especially in urban areas. Then again, when they are captured they are unadoptable because of their wild tendencies. This is a rock-and-a-hard-place situation if ever there was one. Neither feral cats nor previously owned ones have good prospects when the authorities finally catch up with them. The odds are that, once captured, they will contribute to the already overwhelming annual feline holocaust.

Of the five million cats that are brought to shelters each year, three and a half million are humanely destroyed because they are unplaceable. Feral cats account for up to 10 percent of this number, while a large proportion of the others have behavior problems—which may be why they found themselves without a home in the first place. Curiously, the number of cat owners who bring their cats to shelters for the express purpose of euthanasia is low compared to dog owners—evidence that many fed-up owners simply opt for the eviction method as a way of dealing with their cat's behavior problems. However interpreted, the annual mortality figures are unacceptable, and something needs to be done. This travesty is the most compelling reason for taking neutering seriously.

Although I have focused on neutering females as a moral obligation, astute readers will have noticed that I have said nothing about the other half of the breeding team. It certainly takes two to tango, and one male can singlehandedly (if that's the correct expression) cause quite a jump in the unwanted-pregnancy statistics within his own home range (which may be several square miles). Thus, neutering males is highly recommended, too. But there are also behavioral reasons for neutering toms, for example, to curb roaming and urine spraying. Who in their right mind would want to own a cat that spent its life scheming to get out on the razzle? It's bad enough with teenagers without having your cat at it, too. Add to these reasons the not-so-endearing ancillary behaviors associated with the tom's way of life, including fighting and mounting females, and most people agree that castration makes an attractive proposition. You don't need a reminder from the vet when your male kitten needs to be fixed. The smell alone will do it.

Some people have to tolerate "tomcatness" in the name of procreation. I refer, of course, to the breeders, but these folks usually know what they are up against and have their own solutions to the problems . . . but not always. The other day I had a couple of elderly women breeders of British Shorthair cats bring in their champion stud for me to look at. The main question that they had related to their stud's aggression toward judges at cat shows, but they also had concerns over what they considered excessive urine spraying. My first thought about the aggression was that it wasn't all that unusual in an unneutered male, but as it turned out, hormones probably weren't much involved in one of his unwanted behaviors. During the course of the interview some other facts came to light. He had been kept in isolation during the sensitive period of development, which I find always causes problems, and had developed anxiety and fear of strangers. Even now things were far from normal for him in terms of his social experiences with people, but it was all part of a stud's life: you play, you pay. His owners had a room set aside for him where he spent all his days. They had him wear a little pair of diapers ("stud pants") whenever he was out of his crate to contain his spraying behavior. However, once inside the crate with his pants off he would spray like a spigot, even more than the breeders thought was normal for one of his persuasion. Another problem was that he would attempt to mount a little spayed female who shared the room with him, so for her peace of mind the two of them could never be loose at the same time.

I felt that anxiety and frustration were at the root of both of his main problem behaviors. To reduce his frustration at being confronted by the spayed female, I asked that they keep her in separate quarters and find a slightly less provocative roommate for their stud. To deal with the problem of his dislike of show judges, I advised systematic desensitization under showlike conditions, enlisting the help of a bowler-hatted judge facsimile (or whatever). I also recommended the anxiety-reducing medication buspirone to complement the treatment program, but I felt that environmental and behavioral solutions were important, too, if long-term success was to be achieved.

I didn't expect the stud's urine marking and urge to mount to disappear (not without neutering, anyway), but I did anticipate that decreasing his level of anxiety would result in less marking and some improvement in his attitude toward judges. On the first follow-up he was doing much better with the urine spraying, but his fear of cat judges was still evident despite attempts at retraining. In desperation, I added Prozac to the treatment regime to facilitate desensitization, and the result was amazing. His spraying stopped entirely, and he started to make headway with judges (although at my request he wasn't actually entered in shows). His owners were jubilant and at the last checkup were looking forward to tapering off his medications and entering him into his first show in quite a while. I cautioned against showing him while on medication, because I thought it would be misleading for the judges and even unethical, but I didn't feel it was wrong to use medication to straighten him out because I believed that his fears were environmentally induced.

Neutering male cats is an extremely effective way of abolishing unwanted male behaviors. You can eliminate roaming, spraying, and intercat aggression in 80 to 90 percent of cats by neutering. The behavioral change may be rapid, occurring within a couple of weeks, or more gradual, taking several months. The likelihood that castration will cause a rapid change in a behavior depends on the behavior in question. Spraying is most often substantially reduced by castration within days of the neutering surgery, but with aggression and roaming about half of the cats take the slow road. It is easy to understand that some behaviors are more sensitive than others to the effects of neutering, but the puzzling thing is why there should be such marked individual variation in response. For the answer to this, we have to turn to the fundamental question of why a male is a male and how male behavior comes about.

The story starts with the genes. It's the old XX versus XY affair—a matter of chromosomes. What happens is that unborn XY (male) kittens are exposed to a prenatal surge of the male sex hormone, testosterone, from their developing sex organs (testes). The hormonal surge causes the fetus to develop along masculine lines—from a male blueprint, so to speak. Most relevant from a behavioral point of view are microscopic changes in the cellular architecture of the brain. It is this change that confers typical male behavioral attributes. Its work done, the testosterone levels then subside and will not surge again until around puberty. But even prior to the second surge, at adolescence, males are already behaviorally programmed to be males, and they display rudiments of the full male behavior patterns to come. A prepubertal or castrated male can be thought of as a light that has a dimmer switch but which cannot be shut off entirely. Testosterone has the effect of turning up the light to its full intensity. Removing the source of testosterone by castration reduces the light to a dim glow but cannot extinguish it entirely. The extent to which a male displays male behavior may well depend on the magnitude of the prenatal testosterone surge. This may be genetically determined, but neighboring fetuses may also contribute to the masculinization process by altering the hormonal milieu. A male surrounded by two males may become a "supermale" whose sex-linked behavior is more pronounced. Additional factors that may influence the refractoriness of male behavior include experience and learning. The observation by some that late castration is less effective than early castration in altering male behavior tends to bear this out. It may be that experienced cats, like elephants, never forget.

Typical male mating behavior involves the search (roaming),

battles with other suitors (intermale aggression), courtship (often greeted at first by some aggressive rebuttals), and finally the happy union (everything comes to he who waits). Intromission is quite short, lasting only ten seconds or so, and terminates as the female swats at the male and jumps away. This is not an unreasonable reaction to a mating sequence that involves the female being bitten in the neck and pinned. Also, the male's penis is barbed, which one would imagine would add to her temporary discomfort. For the female, all the pleasure seems to come after the event, when she rolls and squirms in apparent ecstasy as her consort withdraws to a quiet spot to lick his penis (charming). The whole process may be repeated many times before the pair separates and each cat goes its own way. Neutering is not usually immediately effective in preventing mating behavior in males, and some 20 percent will still mount females months after castration. Others never forget the joy of sex, whether the first object of their amorous advances was a female in heat or an old sock. In such instances there may be other pressures that come to bear.

A remote consultation I conducted with a client from New York exemplifies the latter situation. The cat's young owner had sought many solutions to the problems she was having with Rex, but as is often the case, nothing seemed to help. Desperate, she sought my services. Our first contact was by fax and read as follows:

Dear Dr. Dodman,

Rex is a one-year-old male cat, found at one week (I think his parents were wild cats that lived in our apartment complex) and raised with a bottle, and then neutered at six months of age after displaying his first "love" for socks. But neutering did not help. In an apparent effort to simulate sex, he holds a sock in his mouth and repeatedly drags it between his legs. He seems to do this a lot in front of people, although I can't say what he does when he's alone. He makes strange noises, too, when he's in the act. Recently I awoke to find Rex having sex with a sock beside my pillow. When I threw the sock off the bed he jumped down and brought it back up and started again. This happened several times until eventually he became mad at me, and I at him, because it was four in the morning.

In addition, he has become increasingly aggressive after playing, petting, or any sort of contact. He has bitten me very hard during some of these bursts of anger. Once when I was sitting on the floor he even jumped up and bit me on the nose, drawing blood.

He has also begun to cry, starting at dawn. He meows insistently until I get up. If I ignore him for a long while (one hour) he will eventually stop, but the next day it happens all over again. He also meows loudly as I leave, unless I give him some tunafish to distract him, and he starts up again as soon as I get home.

When I am playing with him he sometimes goes through fits in which he desperately wants to suck my fingers and will do anything to get to them. When he does manage to get a finger to suck, it seems to calm him.

Rex has had a lot of household stress since December, when my boyfriend moved out (Rex was quite attached to him). Then on April first I moved to an apartment in New York with two other people. He continued his screaming in the morning and having sex with socks. He has also turned over lamps and broken picture frames, something he had never done before. Eventually he grew accustomed to the two other people in the household, but then I found a permanent apartment and moved again on July first. He was quiet for the first couple of days but then started again with the screaming, the socks, the sucking, etc. What's causing these problems, and what can I do about them? Please help.

Catherine

I called Catherine as soon as I received her fax and we chatted for some time as I explained to her what was going on. First I discussed what I thought was fundamental to the development of many of his problem behaviors, his orphan status. Being orphaned is one thing, I told her, but being orphaned and raised by a member of a different species is something quite different. At issue here is the phenomenon of imprinting, first described by Nobel Prize–winning ethologist Konrad Lorenz. Lorenz found that he became "imprinted" on newly hatched ducks if he was the first large moving object they saw. Essentially they followed him tirelessly, apparently regarding him as their mother. The term used to describe this event is *filial imprinting*—learning to recognize your own parent—and it obviously has some important benefits for survival in the wild, but not too many for a domesticated orphan cat. Catherine had probably imprinted on Rex as his mother figure, a phenomenon that would explain his nursing on her fingers in times of stress. Behaviorists describe the potential consequences of hand-raising kittens as simply "overattachment," but I think this term belies the intriguing process that lies behind it.

Then I told Catherine about another type of imprinting, sexual imprinting, which occurs later in life to help animals form the mental images of future mates. Whoever or whatever is generating relevant signals during this sensitive period will create a lasting impression on the receptive mind, in which the image is stored for future use. In Rex's case, warm and fuzzy socks filled the void and became the objects of his sexual desire. The reason neutering didn't cool his ardor is the same reason castration is not

immediately effective for control of other sexually oriented behaviors: it takes some time for these semiprogrammed, semi-
learned responses to be extinguished.

"That all makes sense." Catherine sighed. "It's a great relief to
find out that I was not somehow involved in his fantasies and that
it's the socks that arouse him in that way."

"Now I have to tell you how to deal with the problems," I said.
"The sock fetish could regress in time, but we'll try something a
little more proactive than just wait-and-see. There are several
possible approaches. You could try limiting his exposure to socks
by keeping them in a closet or hamper. This would eliminate the
source of his fascination and possibly speed up the process of his
learning to forget. Then again you could leave the socks around
but try reducing their 'socks appeal' by some aversive strategy.
For starters, try tumble-drying the socks with lemon-scented
dryer sheets. Cats hate the smell of citrus, so the new odor just
might be aversive enough to put him off. Next you could try
booby-trapping some socks. Attach a piece of black thread to a
pair of socks and attach the thread to a shake can—an empty soda
can containing fifteen pennies and taped shut. Then leave the
socks where he can get them. As he grabs the socks for a session
the can will come tumbling down, preferably onto a hard surface,
and the clatter will be a deterrent against future sock sorties.
Finally, you could try redirecting his amorous interests onto some
more appropriate object, namely, a member of the opposite sex.
Think about getting him a female cat for company. That would
help realign his thoughts and teach him the error of his ways. I
know that getting another cat is quite a commitment, but it is the
ideal solution, providing direction rather than attempting avoidance and correction. I think that this strategy may also help Rex
'think cat' and at least partly address his overattachment to you
and his displaced nursing behavior."

Luckily for me, I had a super client who agreed to all these suggestions, including getting a new kitten. But I still had to advise her regarding the aggression problem.

"Let me just address briefly the subject of his aggression to you before we wind up this session," I resumed. "I'm worried about his pushiness and his refusal to take no for an answer."

"Go on," Catherine said, sounding a little anxious again.

"It's related to a trait called dominance. I usually refer to the situation that develops as the alpha cat syndrome. Although he's very fond of you, he has a streak of dominance in him and wants to be running the show. He's interpreted your kindness as weakness and has an elevated impression of his rank in your household. You have to deal with that by setting limits. Decide on the way you want things to be, set limits, and above all stick to your guns. Don't cater to his crying for attention and don't pet him on demand. Above all, don't give him tuna when he's yelling at you. That just rewards the bad behavior. You have to ask yourself, who's training whom? Remember, you reap what you sow."

When the conversation concluded I felt reasonably certain that Catherine would meet with some success using the approaches we had discussed. A week passed before we talked again, but when we did, Catherine was excited and the news was good. She had already seen a major improvement in Rex's manners, and he was really enjoying the company of the new kitten. His sock fetish had disappeared entirely and he had turned his amorous attentions to his new playmate. Although the term *sexual harassment* might have been applicable to the interest he was showing in her, apparently she could fend for herself and knew how to say no. The finger sucking continued, however, so I provided a little extra advice in this department, but basically things were going as well as I could have hoped and I felt that the story of Catherine and Rex was well on the way to a happy conclusion.

It's amazing how sex seems to get into everything. If you get a new kitten, you have to start thinking about sex almost before you can say "Sigmund Freud." Trying to turn a blind eye doesn't work, either, as the kitten soon exhibits hard-to-ignore behaviors that will mandate attention. By the time kittens are six months old or so, the females start rolling around on the floor, caterwauling, and trying their level best to attract every tom in town. Males correspondingly get wanderlust and start spraying urine all over the place. Neutering is a highly effective method of reducing or eliminating sex-linked behaviors but, as discussed, is not as effective in altering male-typical behaviors as it is in changing female (estrus) behavior (though it does guarantee sterility in both sexes). This raises one more point about the difference between males and females. It's not such a divide as was previously believed. Sexually dimorphic behaviors (behaviors that are typical of one sex or the other) are not the exclusive province of any one sex. Females show sexual aggression, mount other cats, and sometimes spray like toms. The reason for this lack of exclusivity is not known with certainty. It seems likely, though, that both sexes are programmed similarly and that the behaviors that are manifested depend on the brain pathways activated. Activation of male mechanisms in females may have something to do with prebirth changes brought about by testosterone from surrounding fetuses (or perhaps elsewhere). Just as a male fetus sandwiched between two males can become a "supermale," so a female sandwiched between two males can become masculinized. Theoretically, neutering such females may heighten their masculine tendencies by eliminating the source of progesterone, a hormone known for its calming effect. Although this has yet to be demonstrated in cats, enhancement of aggression has been reported in female dogs following neutering.

Whatever the effects of neutering on sex-linked behaviors, it is

Part Three

Compulsive
Cats

Eleven

Lucky the
Wool-Sucking Cat

Sigmund Freud, the pioneer of modern psychoanalysis, believed that many of the psychological problems that burden us as adults have their foundations in infancy and childhood. He classified people into four main types: oral retentive, oral expulsive, anal retentive, and anal expulsive. The oral retentive supposedly was an individual who, deprived of the consolation of adequate nursing opportunities during infancy, went on in later life to develop oral fixations. A similar explanation may well underlie the development of the curious feline condition known as wool sucking.

Wool sucking can present itself in many different ways. Some cats simply suck their own or another cat's hair, mouthing it into tiny wet tufts. Others extend their apparent oral fixation to sucking and kneading woolen blankets or their owner's hair. At this point the behavior closely resembles normal cat nursing behavior, where kneading is a major stimulus for milk letdown. At its most extreme, the oral activity is directed at all kinds of fabric, includ-

ing linen, nylon, acrylic, and some plastics, and involves mouthing, chewing, and even ingestion. Blankets, socks, running gear,
underwear, shower curtains, and shoelaces are typical targets of
this aberrant eating disorder. Some experts refer to the condition
as *pica,* meaning a craving for unnatural food, to describe the condition when it has reached this stage of development. Although
much of the ingested material passes through the alimentary tract
without a hitch, material sometimes gets stuck there, causing intestinal obstruction.

There are two factors involved in the development of wool
sucking. The first is genetic, because this oral tendency is particularly prevalent in certain cat breeds. Oriental breeds, such as Siamese, Burmese, and Himalayan, are distinctly overrepresented in
the demographics of wool sucking. The condition is so prevalent
in these breeds that if someone calls up and says, "Dr. Dodman, I
have a cat that chews holes in blankets," my next question is "Is
your cat an Oriental cat or an Oriental mix?" Sometimes the answer is "I don't know" or "I don't think so," but I always imagine that there is some Oriental influence in these cats a few
generations back.

In addition to a genetic predisposition for wool sucking, there
also appear to be nurtural factors that are important in the development of the condition, notably premature weaning. This second factor is the reason for my next two questions: "When was
your cat weaned?" and "When did you first acquire it?" The
genetic theory of wool sucking and the premature weaning theory
are not incompatible concepts, as there is probably some interaction between nature and nurture that ultimately brings about the
behavior. For example, Oriental breeds tend to nurse for longer
than their mixed-breed cousins, leading to a greater postweaning
drive to suckle. Let's say that Oriental cats normally suckle for
sixteen weeks, and domestic shorthair cats would want to suckle
for eight to ten weeks. Placement of kittens at the usual age of six

to eight weeks would represent early weaning for Oriental cats but not for domestic cats. When a domestic cat is weaned at four weeks of age, however, it still has a strong drive to nurse and may displace that drive into ritualized oral activities. It's all a matter of relativity. (Now I see both Einstein and Freud smiling.)

One steamy July day I was halfway through a busy clinic list of predominantly canine cases when my attention was directed to my next client, who was walking toward me with a cat carrier in her hand. *Good,* I thought, *it's time for a change of pace.* I glanced quickly at the record as I greeted the owner, Sue Bronson, who had just driven up from her home in Pawtucket, Rhode Island. I made a quick mental note of the cat's name, Lucky, and then took the carrier from her and we headed for the consulting room. Lucky was a spayed female domestic shorthair cat that was three years old. I peered through the wire front of the carrier to see a twenty-pound tiger-striped cat that looked a bit like the Cheshire cat from *Alice in Wonderland.* But Lucky was not smiling.

Sue and I sat down at either side of the desk in the behavior consulting room and she put Lucky, still in the carrier, on the desk in front of me.

"I'm having a real problem with Lucky," Sue announced. "She's eating me out of house and home—and I'm not talking about food."

She rummaged in a bag on the floor, intent on finding something. Then she stood up suddenly, displaying a blanket full of holes. It was quite a spectacle. There must have been six or seven six-inch-diameter holes in the blanket, and I could see Sue peering at me through one of them.

"She did this in one day," Sue exclaimed emphatically, "and she eats it all. I never find a trace except in her stool."

She sat down slowly, folded the blanket, and put it back in her bag.

"We've tried everything," she continued. "I work for a veterinarian as a receptionist and technician. Between us, we have tried everything there is to be tried—tranquilizers, vitamins, hair ball medication, punishment . . . nothing works. Got any ideas?"

I gazed thoughtfully at Lucky for a few seconds as I pondered my Freudian theories.

"Yes, I do, and I think I may be able to help you and Lucky," I said. "The name given to this condition is wool sucking. It is a rather strange condition that seems to derive from nursing behavior. Let me ask you a few questions about Lucky before I give away too much more. I don't want to influence your answers."

"OK," Sue said as she sank back into the chair. "Fire away."

"First," I said, "do you know if Lucky has any Oriental cat relatives?"

"No, I don't," came the reply. "I don't know anything about her origins because she was a found cat."

"Well, we've drawn a blank there. What age was Lucky when you obtained her?" I continued.

"I don't know that for sure, either," Sue replied, "but I do know she was very young. I would say she was probably about four weeks old. Some passers-by found the litter deserted under someone's porch and figured that the mother had been run over because there was a main road close by. They brought the whole litter to the veterinary clinic where I work. I felt so sorry for them I just had to do something, so I adopted this one. The vet told me that her early weaning could have caused this condition. Do you think that's right?"

"I do," I concurred. "When did you first notice there was a problem?"

"When she was less than a year old. The first odd behavior I noticed was that she would nurse on my dog's nipples. She still does that. The noise is so bad that it wakes people up at night. You hear her slurping and sucking. I wake up and yell, 'Knock it off, Lucky,' and she runs and hides, if I'm lucky."

"So you saw some aberrant nursing behavior when she was only months old. But when did she first start mouthing woolen things and other fabrics?"

"She was about one year old when the fabric chewing started in earnest, and since then she has become progressively worse. Now she is absolutely horrible, as you can see." She gestured toward her bag. "I can't leave her alone in the house at all. I have to shut her away in the cellar. When I'm there, I can keep my eye on her and prevent her from chewing things, but every time I go out I come back to find more destruction. The cellar is the only safe place."

"What do you feed her?" I asked.

"Premium cat food," she said. "I give her a large bowlful twice a day and she eats it all up. She seems to like it. Why, is that a problem?"

"Maybe, maybe not," I said. "But let's talk about diet as a factor in this condition. One of the theories about wool sucking is that affected cats have a craving for high levels of fiber in their diet. Though I don't buy this theory completely, the fact is that when you feed these cats certain high-roughage food it does have a palliative or even normalizing effect. Personally, I think high-fiber diets are effective because they serve to redirect the cat's craving onto a more acceptable target rather than eliminate the compulsion. But if the plan works, who cares? I think it would be worthwhile to try some dietary manipulations anyway. After all, switching diets is a fairly simple and noninvasive fix, if it solves the problem."

To give Sue some idea of the results that can be achieved by dietary measures alone, I told her about another client of mine who had a nine-year-old Siamese cat that had been eating all kinds of paraphernalia for at least seven years. The owner of this cat was beside herself when she came for the appointment. The animal ate a vast array of household items but, as is often the case, wool, acrylic, plastic, and shoelaces were the preferred deli-cacies. Although this owner was resigned to much of the destruc-tive behavior, there were some things that to her were sacrosanct, including her running gear and some other favorite apparel, which she carefully kept shut away inside a wicker hamper. When her cat chewed through the strap that secured the hamper and pro-ceeded to demolish her Nike shirt, shorts, and shoelaces, it was the last chapter in a long saga of half-eaten shower curtains, tat-tered towels, and perforated pantyhose. This was not just another binge, it was a personal violation.

A few days prior to hearing this tale of woe, I had been speak-ing with some fellow behaviorists about wool-sucking cats and these cats' depraved appetites. One extolled the virtues of feed-ing roughage in the form of uncooked chicken wings to these delinquent cats. The other agreed with the roughage concept but preferred chicken necks to minimize the risk of intestinal per-foration by splintered chicken bones. There is one not-to-be-forgotten caveat: *Cooked* chicken bones from any part of the bird are potentially lethal. Uncooked bones, on the other hand, are reasonably safe, because the proteins have not been denatured by cooking and the bones tend not to splinter. When you think of it, cats eat birds in the wild and none of them come precooked. This said, I had one wool-sucking cat referred to me via another behav-iorist that required surgery to remove a (presumably cooked) chicken neck bone from its intestine. For this reason—which is perhaps just a superstition—I personally have reservations about chicken-type treatments.

The dialogue between us behaviorists drifted toward the alter-native of employing a prescription high-fiber feline weight reduc-ing diet. We agreed that this sounded like a reasonable and safe solution. This conversation inspired me to inquire in some detail about the eating habits of our friend the Nike cat. As it turns out, this cat had been fed canned food of a gruel-like consistency for years because the woman's vet had warned that dry food could be a contributing factor in so-called feline urological syndrome. Deprived of food he could really sink his teeth into, the Nike cat would almost kill for a dry food treat. Putting two and two together, I figured the high-fiber diet would be worth a try. I recommended a dry version of the high-fiber food and suggested that the bowl be kept full at all times to provide a more palatable alternative to shower curtains and acrylic whenever the mood came over him. The plan worked like a dream. Given the choice between plastic and dry food, this cat made the sensible choice. I tested our hero's resolve by presenting him with a previously irresistible challenge on the third day of his treatment program. I arranged for his owner to leave a rolled-up pair of running socks in the middle of the living room floor. She reported to me that he gazed at the socks for a moment with a distant expression on his face and then sauntered off disdainfully, as cats do so well. According to his owner, this historic moment heralded a new no-chew era. After seven years of household destruction, the plague was over, or at least diverted.

Sue looked at me a little suspiciously as I concluded my story.

"But I'm already feeding Lucky dry food. Do you think that the switch to high-fiber food will be as effective in Lucky's case?"

"There's only one way to find out," I said.

Sue nodded her understanding. I finished up the paperwork and discharged Lucky, giving Sue written instructions on how to proceed. The advice included avoiding discipline for what I perceived as an intrinsically uncontrollable behavior. Also, I suggested that Lucky should be removed as far as practicable from any potential sources of temptation. I also suggested that Sue should try to reintegrate Lucky into the household as soon as possible because I thought that Lucky's troglodytic life was far from ideal and could have been contributing to the problem by increasing her anxiety level.

Sue tried the dietary solution to Lucky's problem for a couple of weeks and then returned to the clinic for a follow-up appointment. The news was not quite as good as I had hoped, but it was reasonable. Sue estimated that Lucky had improved by about 80 percent. As on the previous occasion, the improvement was rapid, having an almost immediate effect. Sue was beginning to feel more comfortable about leaving Lucky upstairs unattended when she went to work, and she had left the cellar door open almost every day since her appointment with me. Lucky had indulged herself on only one or two occasions, which in absolute terms was a major improvement, but Sue was still uneasy about the prospect of losing even one sweater or blanket per week to this oversized moth. I could see her point.

"Isn't there anything else we could do to improve her a bit more?" she asked. "I don't mean to sound callous, but I'm not sure I can continue to keep Lucky if the behavior persists. It's really getting to me."

I racked my brains for a solution. Then it came to me. Perhaps I should be treating Lucky's problem as a type of compulsive behavior. I called my colleague Lou Shuster for a conference. Lou and I had done a lot of work in the past using endorphin blockers to treat repetitive behaviors in horses and dogs, and I wanted to get his opinion whether treatment with one of these drugs, or an antiobsessional drug such as Prozac, made sense. Lou was very interested by the problem and we discussed the various possibilities. Eventually he said, "Why not try the narcotic antagonist first? At least it will work quickly. You should find out within days whether it's helping. The other way round may take longer than this client has patience for."

He had a good point. If I treated Lucky with a Prozac-like

drug, it could take weeks to find out whether the treatment was successful, but with an endorphin blocker I would know within days. I hung up the phone and turned to Sue.

"With your permission, I'm going to treat Lucky with an endorphin-blocking drug called naltrexone," I said. "It will block the effect of endorphins on her behavior. Endorphins are nature's own morphinelike substances. The brain releases them to reward us for activities that are beneficial for survival, including eating, sex, and exercise. There is evidence that endorphins are involved in the regulation of appetite, increasing the amount of food consumed. People with compulsive eating disorders, such as chocolatoholia, may have excessive release of these brain chemicals, because some have had this compulsion curbed with endorphin-blocking drugs. I have never prescribed endorphin blockers for wool sucking before, but they're safe and we have nothing to lose. So do you want me to give this treatment a try?"

Sue nodded. I explained to her that I might need to switch treatments if naltrexone was ineffective, but I did not go into the details of any other medication at that time. I spent the last few minutes of the consultation giving Lucky a quick physical examination and evaluating her temperament. I noticed that Lucky was rather timid; Sue confirmed this impression by volunteering that Lucky hid whenever strangers came into the house. I wondered if this was genetic or a product of her early weaning.

A week later Sue called up to tell me of Lucky's progress. There had been some minor improvement in the condition, enough to convince me that the naltrexone was having some effect, but it was not the dramatic turnaround for which I had hoped. All in all, I was a little disappointed, but I resolved to persevere for a while longer. The following week Sue reported back to me again, and this time I could tell that she was really disappointed. Lucky had destroyed her favorite shawl and had once again been relegated to the cellar. I decided to switch treatments and talked to her about Prozac-like drugs and how they might help. She wanted to know the rationale behind such treatment. I explained that wool sucking was in many ways similar to obsessive-compulsive behavior in people, and that if the analogy held true, Lucky should respond to antiobsessional medication. She was curious and elected to have Lucky treated this way, for a while at least. I ended up prescribing Anafranil (which has a similar action to Prozac) because I was more familiar with the dosing schedule for this drug in cats at the time. The prescription was phoned in to her local pharmacy so that she could start treatment right away.

Ten days later Sue called me back to tell me that the Anafranil was working well. Lucky was out of the doghouse, and the blankets, clothing, and curtains were safer than they'd ever been. The only area of weakness remaining—Lucky's Achilles heel, so to speak—was shoelaces. Lucky could resist everything except this ultimate temptation, but to Sue, this residual problem was tolerable. She just thanked her stars that all she had to look out for now was laces. After this, several weeks went by and I didn't hear from Sue. I was just beginning to wonder what had happened to her when she called again. She was still happy and Lucky was still doing extremely well, but in the meantime there had been a minor relapse, which Sue had managed herself by raising the dose of Anafranil a hair. This slight dose increase had had the desired effect and the behavior had ceased once more, this time including the shoelace eating. This response was better than I had hoped for in my wildest dreams, and I was grateful for the encouraging success.

I have had several other wool-sucking cats respond to antiobsessional drug treatment since my success with Lucky. One recent case, a beautiful orange shorthair cat called Monty and his sister Mimi, provides an interesting study. Both these cats, who lived together, were described as compulsive plastic eaters. Monty was particularly bad and for two to three months prior to the appointment had escalated the frequency of his licking, chewing, and swallowing of plastic until it was almost continuous. Curiously, plastic eating was not the main reason for the consultation. The appointment was made because Monty had developed a nasty spraying habit and was clearly under a lot of stress. Outside cats were part of his problem, but he was also stressed out by some goings-on inside the house, notably some conflict with a third cat, called Mildred. The plastic-eating problem was a secondary concern for Monty's owner, who had begun to think seriously about whether she could still keep Monty, who was spraying new and more distressing places each day. Spraying was the main problem, so that was what we concentrated our treatment program on. Treatment included keeping outside cats away using aversively scented crystals (aversive to cats, that is). Also, the two squabbling cats were separated, with instructions to reintroduce them gradually by means of a systematic desensitization program. Because of the gravity of the situation, I came out with all guns blazing and, in addition to the above treatment, prescribed Prozac to reduce Monty's anxiety level. Almost as an afterthought, I switched Monty's diet to a high-fiber one to deal with the secondary problem of plastic eating.

My resident, Jean DeNapoli, rode herd on Monty's case after the appointment, and by all rights he was doing fabulously, not spraying at all. According to his grateful owner, we had saved his life. Accolade doesn't get any better than that. Relieved, I asked Jean how the plastic eating was doing, but in all the excitement she had forgotten to ask, so I called myself. It was two months after the appointment when I got around to calling Monty's owner, Claire.

"I understand that Monty's spraying has subsided now, but wouldn't you know it, Jean forgot to ask you about the plastic chewing. How's that doing?" I asked.

"Completely cured," came the reply. "He doesn't touch plastic at all now."

"That's excellent," I said. "So we can chalk up another success for Prozac!"

"Not so fast," Claire said. "I believe it was the diet switch that cured the plastic-eating problem, not the medicine. I have them all on the high-fiber diet now, you know."

Hmmm, I thought, *she might have a point*. But then I asked, "How about Mimi? Has she stopped, too?"

"Why, no. Now that you mention it, she's still at it. Oh, my goodness, it must be the Prozac that's doing it. I hadn't thought of that until this minute."

Recently I have begun to complement pharmaceutical treatment of wool sucking (and plastic eating) with environmental enrichment because I believe environment and lifestyle have a lot to do with propagating the problem. Schemes such as providing cat toys and encouraging more interactive play are intended to defuse environmental tension and facilitate the withdrawal of medication at the earliest opportunity. I need more data before I can draw firm conclusions about the efficacy of these supportive measures but feel sure they will provide some additional benefit.

The results of pharmaceutical treatment are gratifying and tend to indicate that wool sucking might be a feline form of obsessive-compulsive disorder (OCD). This interpretation has to be viewed with some caution, though, because a response to Prozac is not proof positive of an OCD link. Stuttering in humans, for example, responds to treatment with antiobsessional drugs such as Prozac, but stuttering per se is not generally regarded as a form of OCD. Another objection to the interpretation of wool sucking as a form of OCD is that it doesn't bear much superficial resemblance to the supposedly equivalent human condition. There's no doubt that it's a bit of a stretch to go from wool-sucking cats to people who wash their hands scores of times a day or who have exaggerated concerns about their personal safety. Biologically, however, a case can be made for a link.

Many behaviors that are essential for an animal's survival, such as predatory behavior, fear responses, and feeding behavior, are to some extent hardwired in the subcortical regions of the brain. Experimentally, such behaviors can be activated by stimulating specific brain regions with minute electric currents. The result of this direct stimulation is discrete, automatonlike behavior. If the influences normally inhibiting such behaviors were somehow disrupted (say, by chronic stress or anxiety), then the behaviors would be replayed mindlessly. It may be that something like this—central brake failure, if you will—is behind the expression of compulsive behaviors. If this is so, there would be no reason to believe that innate mechanisms governing concerns over personal safety would be the only ones affected. It stands to reason that other innate behaviors, including eating behavior and even sexual behavior, might be affected, too.

There are other criticisms of likening animal compulsions to human OCD that revolve around animals' presumed inability to obsess (and our inability to appreciate it even if they do), but even this point can be addressed. Obsessive-compulsive behavior in children is perhaps nearest to what we see in animals and provides a more illuminating comparison than the complicated adult form of OCD. Pediatric OCD involves repetitive activities of a more elementary form, sometimes driven by obsessions and sometimes not. So obsessions are not necessarily needed for a condition to be accepted as a form of OCD—that seems to dispense with that objection. Whether cats feel bad about what they're doing (as adult humans do) is another matter.

The question remains, are cats such as Lucky obsessed with

their oral predilection, or do they just engage in it mindlessly and automatically as a release from life's tensions? Are potential sufferers programmed at birth, or does early maternal deprivation bring about the problem? No one knows the answers to these questions at present, but new pieces of the puzzle, as they become available, will eventually fall into place and permit the true picture to emerge. One wool-sucking kitten reported to me engaged in wool sucking while it was nursing. That's a strike against the Freudian theory and a home run for those who favor a genetic (perhaps OCD) explanation. But I believe that the factors can operate either independently or together, so there's room for negotiation. Some cats may have such a strong tendency to engage in the compulsive behavior that they are pretty much guaranteed to express it whatever happens. Others with a similar but weaker tendency may never show the behavior unless environmental pressures become intense. A condition like this is difficult to pinpoint genetically, but in time, and with the present rapid rate of development of genetic technology, I feel sure that all will be revealed. In the meantime, at least we now know how to treat the condition, and cats such as Lucky can live to fight another day. He is still alive and well at the time of writing, and yes, he is still receiving his medication and leaving shoelaces and shawls alone. What has changed a little since Lucky's initial appointment is a burgeoning of interest from the medical community in animal equivalents of human OCD. This interest and expertise have been a boon to us veterinarians, and we are poised for some interesting studies that will help clarify the origins of wool sucking in cats and other compulsive behaviors in cats and other species.

in a cat that belonged to a veterinarian friend of mine, Dr. Bob Fleishman, whom my wife worked for at the time. Bob's cat, a rather nervous five-year-old calico called Gabriella, began to strip her fur out immediately after Bob adopted a second cat. The new cat was not of the same disposition as the calico, being somewhat truculent and bossy. As it strutted around its new abode making itself at home, Gabriella hid, and the licking saga began. It is not hard to envisage the stress that Gabriella was experiencing. Imagine being forced to live with an obnoxious person whom you absolutely detested, and there was no way out of it. Wouldn't that be enough to make anyone pull their hair out?

In cats and other animals, the result of being subjected to unresolvable dilemmas is often some sort of displacement behavior. These occur when diametrically opposed behavioral drives conflict with approximately equal intensity. The result: the sudden appearance of a third behavior that is apparently irrelevant and out of context. A good example of a displacement behavior that I heard of from my colleagues at the vet school in Guelph, Canada, involved a working police dog. The dog was trained to attack on command and to break off the attack when the target felon put his hands above his head. One night the dog was on patrol with his handler when they came across a burglar inside a furniture store. As the policeman entered the store, the trespasser, framed in the flashlight beam, was lumbering toward them with a chair held high above his head. The man's intention was to inflict grievous bodily harm, so the policeman gave his dog the attack command. But now the dog was caught in the proverbial cleft stick. How should he respond to two simultaneous but diametrically opposed signals? Should he follow the verbal command and attack or the visual signal and back off? The result was that he did neither. What he did do was to blow a fuse (metaphorically speaking), and he began to spin in circles while the fray went on.

The poor dog never did fully recover from this experience and ended up at the funny farm for dogs, unemployable and continuously running in huge figure-eight patterns as if haunted by the ghostly memories of the fateful day.

Displacement behaviors themselves are not abnormal, though occasionally when circumstances are right (or wrong, depending on how you look at it) they can become a permanent or at least semipermanent feature of an animal's behavioral repertoire. Remember when you were young and your mother would say, "If you keep making that face, it will freeze like that"? It's a bit like that with some of these repetitive behaviors. My cats displace into self-grooming from time to time when they are confused, but never as severely as the dog I described, and they do snap out of it. It often starts when I run into a room quickly and then stop suddenly to weigh my options (which I do all the time). They look at me in part horror, part amazement, and then develop their characteristic perplexed look. I always imagine they are trying to decide whether I am coming or going and are weighing whether to approach in the hope of being petted or to run and hide. In the end the decision becomes too much for them to handle and they displace into apparently nonchalant grooming (like people filing their nails while they wait for the result of an important test). The difference between my cats' behavior and Gabriella's is that mine do eventually stop when the stress (me) has gone, whereas Gabriella kept on going. This persistence on Gabriella's part might have had something to do with her more sustained exposure to the stress-promoting situation, or it might have stemmed from her nervous temperament, which made things seem much worse than they actually were. Whatever the explanation, Gabriella's licking had a life of its own, fueled by some irresistible urge. At this point I felt the behavior could be appropriately described as an obsessive-compulsive disorder. Gabriella kept licking over the weeks following the rude invasion and eventually began to look like a plucked chicken. That was when Bob called me.

"What can we do about this problem, Nick?" Bob asked. "I know that it has something to do with the stress of having the new cat around, but I don't want to give the new guy up because I like him and he needs a home. I've tried desensitizing Gabriella to his presence but that hasn't worked. What else can I do? Do you have any suggestions?"

"Maybe," I mused, mentally conjuring up some earlier positive resolutions to stress-related problems, "but there are no guarantees. This would be a first if it worked."

"I'm ready to try anything," Bob said. "We can't go on like this. Something has to be done."

"I think a good first step would be to medicate Gabriella with an endorphin-blocking drug, such as naltrexone. I have used this drug with success to stop all kinds of repetitive behaviors in horses and dogs and have some limited experience with it in cats. Recently I tried it in a wool-sucking cat and it appeared to be working a bit at first, but with psychogenic alopecia, which is even more clearly stress-related, I think it would be a much more successful proposition. Endorphins are always thought of as stress hormones, but they also function as part of nature's intrinsic reward system, and they regulate grooming as well, so there are several ways that endorphin-blocking drugs could help with Gabriella's behavior."

"I vote we try it," Bob said, and the wheels were set in motion.

Although the theory behind the treatment was elementary, actually giving the medicine was extremely difficult. Each pill had to be divided, crushed up, and somehow administered to Gabriella, and this medication tastes disgusting. For this reason it is difficult to persuade autistic children, some of whom apparently benefit from naltrexone treatment, to take the medicine. The taste is so bitter that it is impossible to mask, even in highly flavored bases. (Sustained-release implants are now being developed for use in children to circumvent this problem.) Somehow, despite the taste, Bob and his wife managed to get the medicine into Gabriella, initially at least. I later learned that it was mainly Bob's wife, Sandy, who deserved the credit for this amazing feat.

One month later I heard back from Bob. There was mixed news. I asked for the good news first and was told that Gabriella's licking had decreased substantially and that she was now sporting new hair growth in the previously bald areas. This was what I wanted to hear. And the bad news? You guessed it—Gabriella had wised up to the treatment and could no longer be caught when it was time for her medicine. The Fleishmans decided that enough was enough and that they would just have to live with a bald cat. I had no other treatment to offer at the time, so they just had to go back to the previously unsuccessful desensitization program designed to enamor Gabriella of her new housemate and hope for the best. We all hoped that one day she would come to accept the usurper's presence and become furry again.

I didn't talk with the Fleishmans about Gabriella's problem for some years after that, assuming that things were much the same. When I did eventually get around to enquiring how she was doing, Bob told me that she had continued to lick herself and had never regrown a healthy coat despite their attempts at rehabilitation. Unfortunately, Gabriella finally succumbed to a renal problem and is now at peace, her worries behind her. Ironically, her nemesis developed psychogenic alopecia a short while after her death. Could he have been missing her? Two cats with psychogenic alopecia in one house—what are the odds against that?

As time went by I saw more and more cats with psychogenic alopecia. Now cognizant of the difficulties involved in administering naltrexone, I sought other therapeutic solutions. Because of the success I had had treating other feline compulsive behaviors with antiobsessional medications such as Prozac, I decided to give this approach a try. I realized that my critics would be at my heels for again reaching for a pharmacologic solution, but I did not believe that any other strategy was likely to be successful. If the condition was at all like human OCD, no amount of retraining was going to solve it. In people with OCD there are two therapeutic strategies, cognitive therapy and medication. Not having much faith in cognitive therapy for cats, I opted for environmental enrichment and medication.

One of the first patients I treated using the then new method was a seven-year-old domestic shorthair called Annabel. Annabel, who had been hand-raised by her owner, Suzanne, was known to be an anxious cat and was easily agitated, so the stage was set. In Annabel's case, two distinct lifestyle traumas were involved in the initiation of the compulsive licking. The first was the loss of her closely bonded cat friend, Tibby, who had had to be put to sleep about a year earlier because of a worsening chronic illness. When Tibby did not come back from the vet's, Annabel wandered around the house for days yowling in misery. Although not intended by her owners, insult was added to this psychological injury by the addition of two new cats to the household a short while after this. The new additions, two sibling kittens, were kept separate from Annabel for about three weeks and then slowly introduced to her. This gentle introduction process did not work. Right from the get-go Annabel always became extremely agitated and hissed loudly whenever she saw them. This was when the licking started.

Annabel continued to lick herself almost incessantly after the kittens' arrival. Her attentions were focused most intently on her left foreleg, hindquarters, and ankles. The licking behavior occurred day and night but was somewhat more intense in the morning and evening, possibly because the middle of the day and the night were quieter and less stressful for her. The only longish respite she had from the self-licking came when the local vet put her on Valium for a while. During this anxiety-reducing treatment Annabel licked less and her hair started to grow back in, but Suzanne was very concerned about Valium, because she knew of its addictive properties, and wanted to get Annabel off the drug as soon as possible. When the Valium was discontinued Annabel's licking resumed at its original intensity and the modest improvement in her coat was forfeited.

Annabel was quite bald and most unhappy when I first saw her. The kittens had grown up and were relentlessly pursuing her around the house, so she had become a closet recluse. The shell shock of her adverse experiences with them had now generalized into a dislike of all cats, and she would become frantic at the sight of any feline, friend or foe. Life was not good. Naturally I conducted a thorough physical examination of Annabel and had a full dermatological workup performed by our staff dermatologist. The results of these tests confirmed the diagnosis of psychogenic alopecia by default. In terms of treatment, there was not much that I could do about the social scene in the house; the new cats were there to stay. What I could change was Annabel's reaction to the twins using a safe, nonaddictive medication, one that I believed Suzanne would find more acceptable than Valium. The drug I selected was Anafranil. This drug, like Prozac, is a potent serotonin-enhancing drug effective in depression and obsessive-compulsive behavior in people. Being cautious, I initially prescribed a very low dose.

The first follow-up by telephone at about three weeks was encouraging but left room for improvement. Annabel had completely stopped hissing and growling at the other cats, but the licking had not changed much. I figured that if the conflict was less, the resolution of the problem was not far behind. I did have to increase the dose a couple of times to achieve the desired effect and at one time had it slightly too high. The paradoxical effect of this surfeit was that Annabel spent all day hiding under the bed. It was as if she had become paranoid. Prozac and its cousins do seem to cause restlessness and anxiety if the dose is cranked up too rapidly, and that seems to be what happened here. On readjusting the dose of medication, this side effect diminished and Annabel's licking continued to decrease. Her hair grew back after a few weeks and she was never seen licking her limbs or trunk while on the medication. She did pay some attention to her tail, however, which to me meant that the behavior had been suppressed and not eliminated.

After one year of treatment, Annabel was brought back to the clinic sporting a luxuriant growth of hair along her flanks and right down to her paws. There was, however, still a little thinning area on her tail where she continued to lick on occasion. Despite this, Suzanne was pleased with her progress. The only concern she had was that Annabel was still spending some time hiding in cupboards. I wondered what would happen if I took her off medication. Would the licking resume at its former level, and would Annabel's personality become more outgoing? Suzanne agreed to try to wean Annabel off medication. The result of this process was, as I suspected, that Annabel's licking returned full force, but she did become a lot friendlier. I was not worried about this, although the relapse potential of these medications does seem to worry some of my colleagues. Obsessive-compulsive disorder in human patients also tends to recur when medication is withdrawn. This does not mean that Prozac and similar drugs are not appreciated by those treated with them; neither does it negate the usefulness of this line of treatment. One and a half billion dollars in annual sales of Prozac bears striking testimony to this statement. What worried me more was the hiding in cupboards that accompanied treatment. This implied that Annabel did not feel all that great about her new life, and I thought this would be a serious drawback to the use of Anafranil in future cases. As it was, it was enough to put me off prescribing Anafranil again for Annabel, so I switched treatment to another anxiety-busting drug, buspirone. On buspirone, Annabel was happy and relaxed and her licking was reduced though not completely abolished. This was the best I could accomplish for her, and I decided to leave it at that.

I dealt with another case of psychogenic alopecia through our remote referral service for veterinarians, called Vetfax. The case involved a nine-and-a-half-year-old American Shorthair called Taylor. True to form, Taylor's owner, Lee, described the cat as a shy, timid animal that was affectionate with those she knew. She was particularly close with one of the other cats in the house, Maddie. Taylor's licking problem started when Maddie came back from the vet's office after major surgery with her body shaved bald from her front legs to her rump. It appeared that Maddie's altered appearance (or, perhaps more likely, her altered odor) caused Taylor some anguish and that this triggered her early desultory licking. At first the licking and hair loss were confined to a small area over one hip. But then a catastrophe occurred. Maddie succumbed to her illness and died. Poor Taylor was beside herself. Her licking intensified, and bald spots began to appear inside her front legs, on her abdomen, and on her tail. The vet ruled out medical causes and tried a shot of long-acting steroid to see if that would help. It didn't. Taylor continued to lick. And that's where I came into the picture. My advice was for Lee to minimize environmental stress for Taylor and to spend as much time with her as possible. The primary cause of the problem could not be addressed, however, as Maddie was gone for good. Medicine did seem to be the most humane solution to Taylor's misery, so I started therapy with an antidepressant right away. I chose Anafranil and hoped I wouldn't see the same side effect I had seen with Annabel. Taylor's licking started to improve after only two or three weeks, and her hair started to grow back in. There were a couple of problems, however. One was that Taylor developed an aversion to the bitter taste of her medicine and would run away from her owner when it was time for her medicine. The second was that Taylor developed the recluse syndrome. We decided that enough was enough, and Taylor was taken off medication. She became more affectionate again but, as in Annabel's case, the licking returned. Lee asked her local vet to represcribe Anafranil. The funny thing was that this time the licking stopped completely and in fairly short order. Not only that, but when the medication was discontinued, Taylor's improvement was sustained. Lee was delighted when I called for a long-term follow-up five months later.

"How can we ever thank you?" she said.

"I'm just happy things worked out for Taylor, but you might want to keep us in mind if any other problems arise," I quipped.

"Well, there *is* something, now that you mention it. It's the new kitten, you see. He's started to urinate outside the litter box, and . . ." Off we went again.

Now, after many successfully treated psychogenic alopecia patients, I have begun to gain confidence in the Anafranil treatment. Not every cat has responded as well as Annabel and Taylor, but most have showed some reduction in licking and experienced a healthy regrowth of their fur. Not all the cats on treatment end up hiding, either. Some show no side effects at all, and others seem happier.

The treatment aspects of the condition are one thing, but

knowing exactly what's going on is another. Do these cats really have a feline form of OCD, or is it just a lookalike condition? It's all very well to talk about psychogenic alopecia as a feline form of OCD, but is the similarity more than skin-deep? Obsessive-compulsive disorder, as it affects people, classically encompasses a fairly narrow range of conditions that involve unreasonable concerns over personal safety or hoarding (the true legacy of a hunting-and-gathering species). So what about compulsive hair pulling? Where does that fit in? In humans, compulsive hair pulling, referred to as trichotillomania, is classified as an impulse control disorder, which is subtly different from a compulsive disorder. However, the winds of taxonomic change are on the side of those who would view trichotillomania as a form of obsessive-compulsive behavior. Several different compulsive behaviors are now being viewed as a spectrum of related disorders. The list of these putative obsessive-compulsive spectrum disorders is extensive and includes conditions such as pyromania, compulsive gambling, and trichotillomania. This new way of looking at compulsive behaviors is fortunate for us animal types, as it facilitates interpretation of OCD as a trans-species biological phenomenon rather than a uniquely human condition. We will never know whether affected cats are actually obsessing about grooming because any obsessions they may have are inaccessible to us. If you assume, however, that cats with psychogenic alopecia experience similar feelings to people with trichotillomania, obsessions wouldn't be anticipated anyway. The feeling that accompanies compulsive hair pulling in people is not obsession so much as loss of control, and by all accounts the experience is not unpleasant in itself, although its effects can be disruptive.

So why are there so many different forms of OCD? To explain this we have to look to genetics. One of the current theories about OCD is that it is a manifestation of some genetically hardwired behavior gone awry. Some behaviors are so important for survival of the species that they come prepackaged, so to speak. The abilities of baby birds to peck their way out of eggs, marsupial young to find the pouch, and mammalian young to nurse are some examples. Other hardwired behaviors include hunting, foraging, eating, grooming, and sexual behavior. Which behavior is preserved depends on the species in question and the importance of the behavior to that species.

Humans, the hunter-gatherers, have these survival-oriented behaviors encoded somewhere in the depths of the brain. It seems almost intuitive that such behaviors would wind up being performed compulsively in some forms of OCD. When predatory behaviors of hunting, shooting, and fishing become the subject of obsessions we call the affected person an enthusiast, a perfectly reasonable person, even though the families of these individuals may suffer from neglect and the misappropriation of family funds. According to psychiatrists, such obsessions do not warrant a diagnosis of OCD, because the person positively revels in acting out the compulsion and does not feel guilty about the obsession. But neither do all people with obsessive-compulsive spectrum disorders, like compulsive gambling and pyromania. I sometimes wonder if extreme sports fans should be classified as having OCD, too: After all, some people are so obsessed with sports that they live and breathe their passion to the virtual exclusion of life as we know it. In Glasgow, Scotland, where the Rangers and Celtics soccer teams battle it out weekly, there is a famous local song that goes as follows: "He's football crazy, he's football mad, and the football game has robbed him o' the wee bit o' sense he had." And I can testify that this description applies to many people— mostly men—that I have come across. The expression "golf widow" describes another one of the maladaptive consequences of a sports obsession. With OCD it's not what you do, but the way that you do it.

Human gathering instincts gone awry take the form of hoarding, miserliness, or kleptomania, all of which are easier to accept as abnormal behaviors than is sports fanaticism. Because some human OCD sufferers end up with unreasonable concerns about personal safety, using reverse logic it can be extrapolated that concerns over safety became hardwired in us somewhere along the evolutionary road. I suppose hunters had to be careful, too.

So where do cats fit into all this? What behaviors might reasonably be considered to be species-typical, necessary for survival, and therefore likely to be hardwired in them? How about eating? How about hunting? Yes to both. And grooming to remove telltale traces of the last meal? That, too, would appear to provide a survival advantage, because if a cat walks around smelling like yesterday's lunch it is much more likely to attract the unwanted attention of both what it is hunting and what is hunting it. Removal of surface parasites and evaporative cooling in warm climes are a couple of other helpful attributes of grooming.

So what about compulsive eating? Does that occur? Yes, it does. Compulsive eating presents itself as wool sucking or pica. And compulsive hunting (predatory behavior)—does that ever occur as a compulsion? We believe so. This particular compulsion takes the form of compulsive tail chasing in some bored cats. And finally, what about compulsive grooming? Compulsive grooming appears in the form of psychogenic alopecia, and suddenly the whole picture falls into place.

If there are other feline compulsive behaviors that might be traceable to evolutionary roots, it should be possible to predict them from other hardwired behavior patterns shown by cats. Have you ever seen cats licking their lips or noses? I bet you have. These are two of the most common ways in which a cat grooms itself, and these behaviors are stereotyped. From this observation one would predict that compulsive lip licking and nose licking should occur . . . and they do. The former results in an erosion referred to as lip granuloma, whereas the nasal erosions may be part of a syndrome known as eosinophilic granuloma (or rodent ulcer). How about allogrooming, when cats groom each other? Might this behavior be useful in terms of survival of the species, and does it manifest itself compulsively? Yes, it might, and yes, it does. A yet-to-be-registered breed, the Ohos Azules, have a particular propensity toward compulsive grooming of their owners' hair. Some long-haired owners have had to find another home for their cats if they want any peace because the grooming of their own hair goes on day and night. Furthermore, this behavior seems to be inherited in a recessive pattern, as does psychogenic alopecia in at least one other breed, the Singapura. The same mode of inheritance is also seen in the compulsive hoarding (of jewelery and other small objects) shown by some Munchkin cats, a breed of cats that have very short legs. They are actually *real* dwarfs (as in human medicine) suffering from achondroplasia. Do you imagine that bringing things back to the nest might be helpful for survival? I would guess so. Mother cats bring back prey for their young, for a start, and are usually quite conscientious about retrieving itinerant kittens. How about compulsive sexual behavior? I have heard of neutered male cats who masturbate until they go cross-eyed (I exaggerate a little to make the point). Need I say more?

The genetic aspects of these behaviors are twofold. First, the behaviors themselves are encoded in the brain, as alluded to earlier, but also there is the tendency to express these behaviors compulsively in the face of environmental stress. This latter component is extremely interesting, as it paves the way for a better understanding of the conditions and of what might be done to treat them. I believe that an anxious temperament leads to an individual's susceptibility, because all affected patients I have seen have been timid or anxious. This is not to say that the environment doesn't play a role. As mentioned earlier, a combination of nature and nurture is probably necessary for the full expression of OCD.

One peculiar thing about OCD in people and animals is the inconsistent response to pharmacologic treatment. The most generally effective treatment involves the use of serotonin-enhancing drugs, although these drugs are not equally effective in all individuals. Some compulsive behaviors in animals respond best to the endorphin blockers, such as naltrexone, while others respond to treatment with neuroleptic drugs. This enigma has been part of the reason scientists have thought of the various compulsive behaviors as separate entities, an explanation that is correct in the sense that different behaviors have different neural pathways and involve different neurotransmitters. But on another, more fundamental level the behaviors are all similar, and should (for some level of understanding, at least) be lumped together. The commonality is the inappropriate release of species-typical survival behaviors in susceptible individuals in response to stress.

One day I was sitting in my office contemplating these things when I received a call from our press officer, Cristin Merck. She said that she had come across a newspaper advertisement for volunteers to participate in a study of trichotillomania in humans and thought I might be interested. She quickly added that she knew I didn't have the disorder but thought I might like to contact the doctor in charge to find out more. I thanked her for her interest and jotted down the number of the study line. A few days later I called and ended up speaking to Dr. Richard O'Sullivan of Massachusetts General Hospital. After a pleasant conversation about the state of the union and other things, we agreed to meet. My entire behavioral staff was invited to the hospital and we sat in on a few of Richard's consultations. I learned a lot by having patients in front of me who could speak. The one thing that struck me was that all these patients seemed to be or have been under tremendous psychological stress. One person had one alcoholic parent and one sober parent. Unfortunately, the sober parent died when the patient was quite young and she was farmed out to a relative. Still, the trichotillomania did not emerge at that time. It took a few years and some additional pressures before the compulsion materialized. Another affected individual, a beard-pulling intellectual in the extension program at Harvard, noticed that his trichotillomania abated when he went hitchhiking across Canada. Presumably getting back to nature and leaving all the pressures of urban life behind caused this remission. A woman patient went into remission when she went on a cruise, probably for the same reason. When I pointed this out to Richard, he just said that such stresses were ubiquitous and not thought to be instrumental in bringing about compulsive manifestations. I silently disagreed and marveled at how similar the patients were to my cats.

Richard wanted to know if I knew of any animal models of trichotillomania that might shed some light on the mysteries of the human condition. I revealed all, and he was thrilled to learn of this untapped resource. It wasn't long before we were scheming about a collaborative project. For me it was the opportunity of a lifetime. Although Richard was interested in collaborating from the viewpoint of learning something new about OCD in people, that was not at odds with our own objective, to learn more about the condition in animals. We did, however, make it plain that we would not care to participate in any studies that would cause any discomfort to our patients. Thanks to this marvelous research team and well-equipped facility, we now have the opportunity to characterize the changes in the brains of affected cats and dogs using noninvasive diagnostic imaging afforded by magnetic resonance imaging (MRI) and position emission tomography (PET) scans (how appropriate). With the MRI technique, sophisticated X-ray equipment accurately detects small changes in regional brain blood flow, indicating enhanced neuronal activity at well-perfused sites. PET scans provide similar but more-specific information, such as oxygen consumption or the activity of the dopamine neurotransmitter system, through the use of various radiolabeled substrates.

The use of such technology is definitely the way to go in the future. A better understanding of regional brain activity in animals that display compulsive behaviors will benefit both us and our medical colleagues, leading to more than lookalike comparisons between animal and human OCD. We will, of course, share our results with the scientific community so that in the future, medical doctors and veterinarians looking at trichotillomanics and other compulsive patients need no longer pull out their own hair at the frustration of working in the dark.

Thirteen

Twist and Shout

It was another busy day in the hospital. People were bustling down corridors, dodging gurneys and each other. An overhead page continuously punctuated the noise, creating an atmosphere like that of Grand Central Station at rush hour. White-coated clinicians, apparently oblivious to the surrounding bedlam, strode purposefully toward various mystery destinations with animals in tow or stood huddled in small groups, engrossed in conversation. Somehow amid the commotion I became aware that I was being paged.

"Dr. Dodman, please come to B ward. Dr. Dodman to B ward, please."

I had been heading to my office to catch up with some paperwork but made an about-face and headed to the wards. When I arrived in B ward I found a cluster of clinicians and students gathered around one of the stainless steel cat cages. I couldn't identify the subject of their attention at first, but whatever it was, it was arousing considerable interest. One of the students spotted me and cleared a way for me to shuffle forward. I peered into the cage to see an extremely handsome seal point Siamese cat on red alert. The cat was backed into the corner of the cage and sat stiffly, staring out, with its pupils as big as saucers. I had seen this look many times before and knew well that it would be unwise to attempt to handle the cat at this point. On further inspection I noticed that the cat's tail was virtually denuded of hair and looked like a rat's tail.

"Ah, Dr. Dodman," one of the clinicians exclaimed, "thank goodness you're here. This cat was in for medical evaluation of a suspected seizure condition, but I think it has more of a behavior problem. It's really aggressive sometimes and has peculiar bouts when it becomes extremely agitated and hostile. Do you have any idea what could cause this?"

As he was speaking I surveyed the ID card on the cage identifying the inmate as Jean-Paul, a four-and-a-half-year-old neutered male Siamese cat.

"He's just bitten one of the students," the clinician continued. "It was a nasty bite and the student had to go to St. Vincent's for IV antibiotic therapy."

"What was the student doing to get bitten?" I questioned.

"Just petting him," came the reply. "The attack came right out of the blue—no warning at all. Got any ideas?"

"It could be any one of a number of things," I replied. "Is there any chance I could have a word with the owner to find out a little more about this cat?"

"Oh, sure. She's really upset about the student getting bitten. She says it's not like Jean-Paul to go around biting people like this and would like to find out what's going on. She thinks the strange surroundings and all the commotion here agitated him."

"When can I see her?" I pressed.

"Right now, if you have time. She's out front in one of the consulting rooms."

I saw my opportunity to catch up on paperwork melting away, but Jean-Paul's case had riveted my attention and there was no getting away now. I just had to find out more about this rebellious cat and his hair-trigger temper. I headed off to the consulting room, knocked gently on the door, and let myself in. Jean-Paul's owner, Ms. Rogers, was sitting quietly in the room. As I entered she cocked her head to one side and smiled.

"Hello, I'm Dr. Dodman," I announced. "Do you have a few minutes to talk to me about Jean-Paul's behavior?"

"I certainly do," she replied pleasantly. "I've been worried about him for some time and I just have to find out why he's behaving like this."

I sat down, case record in hand, and began to detail his behavioral history. Ms. Rogers knew a lot about Jean-Paul because she had owned him since he was six weeks old. Other than a bout of urine spraying at six months of age, negated by timely neutering, Jean-Paul's history was rather unremarkable. Essentially he had been a perfectly normal cat until April 1, 1993, three months prior to his appointment at Tufts, when he had started his present shenanigans. These took the form of sudden bouts of agitation, which would begin with him flicking his tail from side to side. Then he would jump up with a start and run around frantically (not really going anywhere in particular), stopping at intervals to lick his tail intently. Each attack was over almost as soon as it started, although Jean-Paul would remain aroused for some time afterward, as evidenced by his dilated pupils and frequent twitching of the skin along his back. Episodes like this occurred several times daily, particularly around 4 P.M., 8 P.M., and 3 A.M., and were of great concern to Ms. Rogers. With a little prodding, Ms. Rogers recalled one other strange behavior. Apparently Jean-Paul also chewed compulsively at his back claws and paid an inordinate amount of attention to the base of his tail. Ms. Rogers's local veterinarian had diagnosed psychomotor epilepsy—behavioral seizures—as the primary problem and started Jean-Paul on phe-nobarbital. When this was ineffective he tried steroids and then Valium, all to no avail. He then suggested an appointment with our medicine service at Tufts.

What I had heard so far sounded typical of a condition known as feline hyperesthesia syndrome, a bizarre behavioral syndrome that predominantly affects Siamese cats. The term *hyperesthesia* means "heightened sensations" and refers to a sensitivity to touch that affected cats appear to have along the midline of their backs and sometimes down to the tip of their tail. Stroking a cat with this condition along its back may precipitate a full-blown attack, including agitation, tail twitching, skin rippling, and self-directed grooming. Irritable aggression is also sometimes associ-ated with this constellation of signs. This is probably what caused the student to get bitten.

I still had to decide on a treatment for Jean-Paul's condition. The classic approach is to regard the condition as a type of seizure, as the referring veterinarian had done. In this case an anticonvulsant such as phenobarbital is the logical treatment. However, phenobarbital had already been tried in Jean-Paul's case with little or no success. What now? Should I try treating his condition as a stereotypy, a pointless, mindless, repetitive behav-ior, or should I treat it as a form of obsessive-compulsive disorder? I had no prior experience with either of these approaches at the time and there was nothing relevant in the literature. But I had successfully treated self-directed behaviors in other species on the assumption that they were stereotypies, so this seemed like a reasonable first approach. The licking component of the behavior at least fit the definition of stereotypic behavior, although the other aspects were atypical. The compulsive-behavior theory was an even longer shot because it required the unusual contingency that grooming behavior *and* aggression occur simultaneously.

Because I opted to treat Jean-Paul's behavior as a stereotypy, I selected the endorphin-blocking drug naltrexone as my first choice. I explained the rationale underlying this selection, namely, that if stress-released endorphins were propagating the behavior, they would be neutralized by such treatment, and found that Ms. Rogers was nodding sagely and following every word. She even ventured that Jean-Paul's ticlike movements were reminiscent of human Tourette's syndrome. I was quite surprised by her insight and asked her whether she had a medical background. Then I found out why she was so well informed. She was a school psychologist who spent much of her day dealing with kids affected with attention deficit disorder and other impulse-control disorders. Lucky me. An informed client is always best to work with, especially when novel treatments are involved.

Two weeks later I had my first follow-up conversation with Ms. Rogers. She reported that the intensity of Jean-Paul's attacks was reduced immensely and that he was behaving much more like himself. He had become more playful and was following her husband around the house as he had in the good old days. One thing hadn't changed, however. The attacks were still occurring frequently, about three times a day. I decided to increase the dose of naltrexone to see if I could achieve any further improvement in Jean-Paul's condition. About two weeks later I spoke to Ms. Rogers again only to find there had been very little change. It seemed that Jean-Paul could now be distracted from his aberrant behavior, but it appeared we could not get him to improve beyond a certain point. Ten days later the news was worse. Jean-Paul had relapsed and was going for his tail with his original intensity. He was also doing a lot of grooming, especially around his rear end, and had developed the interesting habit of carrying around a pair of socks and chewing on them at mealtimes in between mouthfuls of food. It was time to engage plan B.

I suggested to Ms. Rogers that we treat the condition as a case of feline compulsive behavior and implement a course of the anti-obsessional drug Anafranil. It didn't take much to convince Ms. Rogers of the similarities between Jean-Paul's condition and OCD, although we both were also aware of the differences. I started Jean-Paul on a low dose of Anafranil, hoping that this would calm him and stabilize his fluctuating moods.

At the one-week follow-up Ms. Rogers reported that Jean-Paul was much more relaxed. He had had only a couple of brief attacks during the entire week, and both Ms. Rogers and her husband were absolutely delighted with his progress. They did notice that he was eating a little less and was standoffish at times, but they thought that this was because of the steamy August weather. I informed her that these changes were probably a side effect of treatment but would most likely fade within a week or two.

A few weeks later I had Ms. Rogers bring Jean-Paul back for a follow-up appointment. His improvement had been maintained and the hair was beginning to grow back on his tail. His appetite was back to normal, he was more playful, and he was beginning to pay more attention to what was going on around him. Before Jean-Paul was taken home I had some photographs taken of his "rat tail" to remind me of our trials. Because of the success of treatment and new hair growth, these photographs were much less dramatic than they would otherwise have been, but I wasn't complaining.

The weeks and months slipped by, and through various follow-up telephone conversations and faxes I learned that Jean-Paul's improvement had been sustained. I saw him twice more on annual follow-ups, and at the latter of these visits, after two years of medication, he was still happy and playful and sporting a full tail of hair. Because of my success in treating Jean-Paul's condition with Anafranil, this drug subsequently became my treatment of choice for cats with hyperesthesia syndrome.

Wolfgang, another four-year-old neutered male Siamese cat who arrived in my office shortly after Jean-Paul, taught me a few more lessons about feline hyperesthesia syndrome. As in Jean-Paul's case, Wolfgang's condition had started precipitously. One afternoon, about a month before his appointment at Tufts, Wolfgang suddenly jumped up as if he had been stung by a bee and ran around looking over his shoulder as though something were following him, pausing occasionally to groom his back with great intensity. He finally hid under a chaise and it was a while before he ventured out. After this, he had two more similar attacks at approximately one-week intervals. The second attack occurred at night, when he was settling down to sleep. This time, his owners reported, he appeared "worried" and his body was twitching. They also noticed that he had a faraway expression, appearing to be in an almost trancelike state, and that he was inconsolable. The third attack was precipitated by a barking dog. The sound caused him to run and hide in a closet, where he remained for some time, pupils dilated, skin twitching, intermittently licking and chewing his back. This behavior sounded more characteristic of a seizure than Jean-Paul's had and rekindled my suspicions that neurologic events were behind the behavior.

Wolfgang also had some other peculiar behaviors. He had shown indications of an unstable temperament for about a year prior to the first real attack. Specifically, his mood would fluctuate from calm and composed to extreme agitation in a matter of seconds. For some time now his owners had considered him to be rather jumpy and easily frightened. They reported also that he experienced excessive hair loss during stressful periods, possibly as a result of excessive grooming, and there were times when he appeared to be seeing things. At these times he would run away from what appeared to be imaginary pursuers, stopping occasionally to lick his back. Now and then he would also sit, looking a little apprehensive, appear to see something descending toward him, duck his head down low to the ground, and then with his eyes follow the path of the imaginary dive-bomber off to the far side of the room. Talk about little green men . . . very strange. I think Wolfgang had suffered from hyperesthesia syndrome for longer than his owners suspected.

The hallucinatory phenomenon was particularly interesting to me. Some years earlier I had seen a videotape of one other cat showing identical signs but didn't have the medical history to go with it and thus was in the dark about its etiology. Because this behavior was so striking, I once showed this videotape at a feline symposium at Tufts and asked the assembled throng of cat owners and breeders whether any of them had seen anything like it. No one had, but one woman in the front row stood up and ventured an opinion about what was going on. She prefaced her remarks by informing the other participants that she was an M.D. (anesthesiologist) and then suggested that the hallucinatory behavior was reminiscent of schizophrenia in humans. She thought that perhaps antipsychotic medication would be the most logical treatment. I had a deep interest in learning more about the hallucinatory behavior but had to wait for Wolfgang to come along until I had a case of my own to investigate. The crowning glory was that Wolfgang actually had one of these dive-bomber attacks right there in the consulting room before my very eyes. What luck!

Working on the OCD theory first, I treated Wolfgang with Anafranil and waited expectantly for the first follow-up report. One month later I was delighted to hear that he was "doing wonderfully." There had been no more incidents of fear or agitation. He also appeared far less anxious and had shown no more twitching along his back or excessive self-directed licking. Even the hallucinations had disappeared. Medicating him was not a problem for his owners, who simply put the powder in his food once daily. Apparently he didn't mind the taste; what a patient! The result of this medication was a cool cat and happy owners. One interesting side effect of Anafranil, which the owners noticed in the early stages of treatment, was excessive tearing, a side effect also reported in people. To control this, I had them reduce the dose of Anafranil slightly. The tearing ceased, but this was the beginning of several concerns that Wolfgang's owners had about the medication. I think the main problem was that they didn't feel comfortable with the possibility that Wolfgang might have to stay on medication indefinitely. This translated into their escalating anxiety to have him weaned off at the earliest possible opportunity. To comply with their wishes, I advised tapering the dose about a month later. Three months after Wolfgang was off medication entirely he was still maintaining a good deal of the improvement he had shown, and although he now occasionally showed skin rippling along his back, at least he was free from full-blown attacks, and he remained so for as long as I was able to stay in touch.

Wolfgang's case directed me to rethink the origins of feline hyperesthesia syndrome and introduced me to the concept of hallucinatory behavior. His response to Anafranil pointed more to an OCD-like condition than schizophrenia. If he had suffered from a schizophrenia-like condition, the hallucinatory behavior might have escalated rather than vanished with his treatment. Nonetheless, I couldn't and still can't completely rule out some schizoid component to his behavior. That thought is still on the drawing board. Wolfgang's case also taught me about a previously undocumented side effect of Anafranil in cats, tearing. All this learning *and* Wolfgang feeling better—you can't do better than that.

With thoughts of these recent treatments in my mind, I set off on a lecture trip to Nevada to deliver a continuing-education lecture at the California/Arizona/Nevada Tri-State Veterinary Meeting. When it came to the subject of repetitive behaviors in cats, I floated my obsessive-compulsive theory of feline hyperesthesia in front of some 150 veterinarians, who appeared to appreciate these recent developments in the management of the condition. Needless to say, the photograph of Jean-Paul's rat tail got a lot of attention. During question time, two seasoned practitioners sitting next to each other in the front row raised their hands to share their experiences with feline hyperesthesia. Both reported seeing cases in which petting along the spine caused the cats to fall on their sides, arch their backs, and paddle their legs. They were describing grand mal epileptic seizures, and we all knew it. I had to acknowledge this corroboration of earlier views on the origins of feline hyperesthesia but had difficulty reconciling this with the apparent success of Anafranil therapy. Theoretically, Anafranil could even precipitate seizures. The only explanation for its success I could come up with was that the drug was somehow preventing outside events from triggering seizures, perhaps by stabilizing mood, but this rationale is entirely homegrown and as yet unsubstantiated. I have, however, successfully treated other partial seizure conditions in dogs with Anafranil, so maybe there's something to the theory.

On my return to Massachusetts I dug up a rather obscure publication on feline psychomotor epilepsy written by a veterinarian named Dr. Barbara Stein. She described three types of psychomotor epilepsy in cats. The first was a condition very similar to what was troubling Jean-Paul and Wolfgang, the second was explosive aggression, and the third was either of the previous two conditions progressing to convulsions. Dr. Stein's splendid report prompted me to recall one or two other cats I had seen that were extremely affectionate one minute, soliciting affection and petting from their owners, then savagely attacking them the next. The fact that these cats may have had a seizure problem was a revelation for me at the time. I assume that the various clinical manifestations of feline hyperesthesia depend on the location of the seizure focus in the brain and how it radiates from there. Discrete and well-contained seizure foci may produce bouts of agitation, excessive grooming, or other abnormal behaviors, whereas a large focus spreading to the cerebral cortex would result in convulsions. Following this line of reasoning, Dr. Stein's description of a primary aggressive form of feline psychomotor epilepsy without progression to a full-blown seizure probably represents a relatively localized form of the condition.

I have been confronted with additional substantiation of the role of seizures in the genesis of feline hyperesthesia syndrome since these early revelations. For example, although Jean-Paul was unresponsive to anticonvulsant therapy, I have seen several cases of the syndrome that were successfully managed with this treatment. Another piece of evidence in favor of the seizure etiology came from a fascinating case that I thought was an example of a different syndrome.

The cat in question, a three-year-old spayed female Siamese mix called Squirt, was brought to me at Tufts in the spring of 1993. Squirt's problem was vicious biting of her own tail, resulting in self-mutilation. Her owner, Vince Pachette, had a tremendous emotional investment in his cat and was extremely concerned.

"You've got to help me, doc," Vince said, choking on his words. "You've got to help me save Squirt. My wife thinks I've taken her to be put to sleep, but I just can't bring myself to do it. We've spent so much money on her already that my wife thinks we should call it quits. After all, we don't seem to be getting anywhere. I want you to answer a question for me before we get started. Do you think there's a chance?"

I looked at Squirt carefully before answering. Although Squirt was fairly alert, she couldn't coordinate her voluntary muscular movements, and she was always falling to one side. She was also rather emaciated, weighing only six pounds. It looked as though a medical condition might be involved, possibly something neurological. The prospects weren't great.

"There's always a chance," I replied, hedging a little, "but I need to check her over before I can say how good a chance."

"Fair enough, doc. I didn't mean to put you on the spot. What do you need to do?"

I explained the need for a thorough clinical examination, and with this understood, I got to work. Things turned out a lot better than I expected. It wasn't too long before I had convinced myself that Squirt wasn't in as bad shape as it first appeared and was treatable. I started asking Vince some questions about Squirt's behavioral history. I learned that Vince first acquired her from a shelter when she was only three weeks old. She had had a grand mal seizure when she was two and a half months old and had been treated with phenobarbital and Valium ever since. She had been unsteady on her feet for as long as Vince could remember, showing poor balance and poor walking and running skills. I wondered how much of this was attributable to the medication she was taking. She still had seizures about once a month, but once a month was livable for Squirt and Vince, and so they went on. The tail biting, which had begun six weeks prior, occurred twice every second day. It was usually preceded by a calm period in which Squirt would be lying down, looking normal, and licking her flank. Then suddenly all hell would break loose for about ten to fifteen minutes. The mayhem involved vicious tail biting that would draw blood, and what Vince interpreted as shrieks of pain. In retrospect, the shrieks were seizure-related and probably a subconscious reaction.

I asked Vince to tell me about a day in Squirt's life to see if I could find out anything that might throw some light on the matter. At the time of this consultation I regarded the problem as a form of stress-induced self-mutilation rather than feline hyperesthesia, drawing on the knowledge I had at the time. I realized that self-mutilation in people sometimes can have genetic roots— for example, in Lesch-Nyhan syndrome, in which children bite off the tips of their fingers or their lips—and that sometimes it can be environmentally induced. Environmental causes of self-directed aggression in people include childhood abuse, leading to borderline personality disorder, and incarceration in prisons or mental institutions. There wasn't anything I could learn about Squirt's genetic background because she had come from a shelter. Likewise, I couldn't pursue her behavioral background prior to Vince's acquiring her. Vince informed me that Squirt had lived like a queen since he had owned her, and that as far as he could remember she had not had any ghastly accidents, such as being dropped on her head. At night she slept on her favorite chair in the dining room; in the morning she arose from slumber to have a gourmet breakfast and then spent the rest of the day lounging around and doing pretty much as she pleased. Vince was the breakfast preparer, and Squirt came running when she heard the sound of a spoon against metal. She would circle Vince expectantly as he hastened to serve up the feast, which typically included any one of a selection of canned cat foods, chicken, liver, beef, or even seafood. Following a hearty breakfast, Squirt would retire to the comfort of her own fluffy throw rug for a few more Z's, or on a sunny day she might catch a few rays on a windowsill in the living room. None of this sounded particularly rough to me, but I wondered whether Squirt was socially deprived. When I asked about this, Vince told me that there was another cat in the house, Samantha, who was good company for Squirt whenever Squirt was in the mood for fun (which wasn't that often). During the good times, the two cats would play together, having fits of the "maddies"—running up and down the stairs and chasing each other around the legs of the dining room chairs. No hostilities ever occurred. Vince reported two other behaviors of Squirt's that made me sit up and listen. The first was that Squirt would sometimes pace around in circles for quite a while for no apparent reason, mimicking her breakfast anticipatory behavior. This sounded a bit compulsive to me. The second was that she loved to spend time on tables and reveled in removing objects, such as lighters and pens, by carrying them off to some remote place in her mouth. This behavior sounded compulsive and smacked a little of the Munchkin cats' hoarding behavior. Although I didn't quite understand the significance of these behaviors, I took note of them for future reference.

From Vince's description of a day in Squirt's life, it didn't seem that there was much I could do in terms of environmental enrichment, so I felt that any intervention would have to be pharmacologic. Naltrexone was my treatment of first choice, since I was dealing with a self-mutilating behavior. I asked Vince to discontinue Squirt's Valium, because I thought it was causing more problems than it was worth, but asked him to continue the phenobarbital because of the cat's epilepsy.

The days ticked by following the appointment, and I kept my fingers crossed for Squirt and for Vince. When the news came it was good. No, it was spectacular. Not only had Squirt ceased the tail biting, but she was no longer uncoordinated. She was like a new cat. I followed up with Vince for many months, and Squirt's improvement was maintained. Vince was delighted and so was I.

That could have been the end of the story—a case of self-mutilation successfully treated with naltrexone—but something kept haunting me about Squirt's other behaviors. I felt sure that all the components of the condition should tie in together somehow. And then it came to me. A Siamese cat, seizures, sudden frenzy and aggression following an episode of grooming . . . could it be that tail biting is a form of feline hyperesthesia syndrome? It certainly seemed so to me, but why had Squirt responded so well to the naltrexone, and where did the circling and hoarding fit in? That was still a mystery.

And what now of the obsessive-compulsive theory? Was it completely dead? The answer was no. There is some common ground between partial seizures and obsessive-compulsive disorder in people, and the same may well be true in feline hyperesthesia. One girl I read about had OCD *and* seizure-induced rage attributed to a discrete seizure focus in a particular part of her brain. When the seizure focus was surgically removed, both the compulsive behavior and her aggressive outbursts subsided. You can find other evidence in the medical literature of a link between OCD and seizures. For example, in one case series, seizures were reported in 10 percent of a cohort of human OCD sufferers. In addition, electrical stimulation of certain regions of the brain produces repetitive behaviors, including grooming and rage behavior. In theory, then, a discrete seizure focus could produce compulsive self-grooming, episodic aggression, and many other behaviors. It could also spread to other areas of the brain, causing grand mal seizures. The type of compulsive behavior produced by a discrete seizure focus would depend on the location of that focus, but manifestations could include compulsive eating behavior, compulsive predatory behavior, and hoarding (to name but a few). The fact that some cats with feline hyperesthesia show more than one abnormal behavior simultaneously is predictable from this hypothesis and represents an overlap of the electrical disturbance between brain regions. Jean-Paul displayed at least two compulsions, excessive grooming and aggression. It is conceivable that his sock-carrying compulsion may also have been associated with his condition. Wolfgang had a few peculiar behaviors ranging from compulsive grooming and hallucinations to skin twitching, kindled by the same (putative) seizure disturbance. Squirt's self-directed aggression, circling, and hoarding also may have been compulsive manifestations of underlying seizure activity.

The only question remaining was why Squirt had responded to naltrexone. This can be explained on the basis of endorphins being involved in the propagation of aggressive behavior. It turns out that endorphins facilitate offensive aggression. Endorphin blockers such as naltrexone are the sexy newcomers when it comes to treating violent human offenders, according to research psychiatrist John Ratey of Harvard University. From Squirt's case we can assume that endorphin involvement applies even if aggression is initiated compulsively and is self-directed. This is a viable explanation for what happened with Squirt.

Jean-Paul, Wolfgang, and Squirt know nothing of the ruminations that go on behind the scenes in our behavioral clinic. All they know (or care about?) is that they feel a lot better since their visit to Tufts. Their owners, too, are delighted that their cats are alive and well and that their aberrant behaviors are at least under control. As for me, I am wondering how to substantiate all these theories and how to develop better diagnostic and therapeutic strategies. Even today when I see cases of feline hyperesthesia I wonder whether to treat them as seizure cases or as compulsive behaviors. My tendency is to treat the problem as a compulsive behavior first, because I have had more success with Anafranil than phenobarbital. Whatever approach I select, however, I find that more and more I am attempting concurrent environmental modification and suggesting improvements in daily management (feeding, exercise, and interactions with the cat) that I feel will be psychologically beneficial for the cat. Compulsive behaviors seem to escalate when stresses abound. Seizures, too, seem to be triggered by environmental events. For both these conditions, therefore, it is prudent to do what can be done to modify life's stresses and to attempt to ensure a peaceful, quiet environment for the cat. What is actually done varies tremendously from case to case. Sometimes, when feuding feeds the tensions, we suggest a program of desensitization to other household cats. On other occasions we change a cat's view of the world by opening and closing various blinds or blocking off windows. Often though, the advice we give is simply to move slowly and quietly around the cat to reduce anxiety and to minimize the stimulation of petting, especially along the spine. Sometimes it is possible to make a major impact with such changes, and some cats may be able to cope without medication eventually, which is of course our (and the owner's) ultimate goal. It's not that such cats are cured; it's just that we've found a way of minimizing stress or eliminating other powerful triggers for the behavior.

A more accurate diagnosis of the exact site and extent of the problem would help to make the treatment of hyperesthesia more rational. At the moment we have to leapfrog from clinical signs to treatment, with the actual mechanism for the behavior a black box that we can only speculate about. Detailed physiological testing would go some way toward resolving the dilemma. Electroencephalography may help but is suspect in animals, so we may have to go upmarket and resort to some of the newer brain imaging techniques, such as metabolic MRI and single photon emission computed tomography (SPECT) scanning, to make the next round of breakthroughs. However appropriate CAT scanning may sound as an imaging technique, it probably would not help much with a functional problem of this nature, but luckily there's more than one way to scan a cat.

century. Why, then, do we let our cats eat their way to early graves without lifting a finger to stop them? Some folks, it seems, do not have the stomach to refuse their cats excessive amounts of food, but that's not the whole story. There are cat factors, too.

Most animals have intrinsic regulatory mechanisms that under normal circumstances determine when they stop eating. Cats are no exception to this general rule. When cats can eat at will, the caloric intake of each of the several small meals they consume daily is approximately equal to that contained in one mouse. Although a number of factors, including the season, environmental temperature, and sex hormones, cause some slight variation in a cat's food intake, this does not explain why some house cats keep eating until they can hardly walk. Talk about shop till you drop—this must be the eating equivalent. There are several possibilities for this apparent enigma. First, there is the diet itself. Many of the processed foods we feed our cats today are compact, energy-rich, and designed to be super-palatable. This permits ingestion of a high calorie load in just a few meals. Second, we have facilitated a major change in our cats' eating habits by feeding them prepared food. Cats no longer have to track down their food and wrestle it to the ground. Getting food is now a rather boring affair accomplished with minimal energy expenditure and little, if any, excitement. In psychological terms, we have eliminated the appetitive phase of their feeding behavior. Most house cats do not have a real job and are inactive for much of the day. Lovable they may be, but busy they are not. When you're neutered and inactive there's nothing more exciting than having "a little something" (as Pooh used to say) to break up the tedium. Genetic factors, too, are involved in the tendency to be overweight. The recent discovery of an obesity gene in rats has certainly put the cat amongst the pigeons in the world of human dietetics. Now I hear that a new strain of lean mice that can eat a lot without gaining weight has been developed in a laboratory in California.

Finally, it seems likely that feline obesity may arise as a result of the anxiety and stress of the modern cat's life. Perhaps the problem starts as displacement eating, a little comfort bingeing from time to time, but if psychic pressures are maintained, the eating habit may then assume the proportions of a compulsion. Cats, like people, may suffer from compulsive overeating as one of a spectrum of obsessive-compulsive disorders.

All kinds of medical as well as physical problems plague the overweight cat, ranging from diabetes and difficulty getting around to breathing problems and cancer. There is no good reason to permit a cat to remain overweight, and in the interest of our pets' health it is best to set some limits. I know that this is not easy, as I have dietary struggles with my own cats and always feel like a traitor when I ration their food. Given the option, my pesky pair would eat almost continuously and gain an inordinate amount of weight. Perhaps they, too, suffer from the indoor cat blues. I always know it's time to do something when the fat pads between their back legs start to wobble when they walk. I have attempted to address this serious problem by cutting down on their food supply, but it's really difficult to withstand their constant begging and food stealing, so now I have taken the coward's way out and started feeding them a weight-reducing diet. This has been a happy compromise for all of us. They have the pleasure of eating substantial quantities of food without the associated risk of turning into a feline Tweedledum and Tweedledee, yet their begging is at a tolerably low level (unless we are having chicken or fish for dinner, which they can smell from forty feet in a northeast gale). They are happy and in reasonable shape, and I have a clean conscience. Thank heaven for diet foods.

The fattest cat I ever saw belonged to my wife's aunt Marsha. Her cat was so huge that it didn't take a genius to figure out that something was wrong. It weighed twenty-something pounds and slept on its back, giving an impression of a beached jellyfish.

Bonker, as this poor cat was called, could hardly move at all. The only indication that the unidentified lying object was a cat came after close inspection of the mass, noting the slow, rhythmic breathing and the flutter of eyelids at the sound of the refrigerator door opening. Needless to say, my wife and I cautioned Marsha about the long-term consequences of maintaining Bonker in such condition, but I'm not so sure she was really listening. Maybe she was right to give us such short shrift, because free access to food may not have been the whole story with Bonker. I gathered from his apparently pointless Hotel California–style existence, masterly inactivity, and overindulgence in sleep as well as in food that he had some psychological problems. It was almost as if he were depressed. I have seen the same signs many times before, notably in some bears at the San Diego Zoo. These bears, despite their keepers' attempts to enrich their environment, slept their days away in their cave, and because of this they weren't often around for visitors to see. Eating was their only pleasure. The solution to this snoozy problem was to distribute their food from a hopper as the tour bus rounded the corner so that sightseers could observe the bears foraging for their chow. Given the choice between sleeping and eating, the bears opted for the latter, thus resolving the keepers' dilemma, though not their own.

The overeating that accompanied Bonker's condition seemed to be part of a similar syndrome that may be related to boredom or frustration. Psychogenic polyphagia, as this eating disturbance is called, causes animals to eat more than they normally would, as a coping mechanism. We have all suffered from stress occasionally, and we know that the cookie jar is a favorite destination at such times. But why would Bonker, apparently living in the lap of human luxury, suffer such inner turmoil? Being a hunter without a quarry, a prowler without a prowl, a fighter without a fight, may have something to do with it. Although we do our best to provide our feline friends with everything money can buy, it seems that what we can't supply, a biologically purposeful existence, is the missing factor that spawns the problem. The result of this type of environmental pressure, at least in susceptible animals, is displacement into any one of a plethora of repetitive behaviors, and compulsive eating is merely one of the potential manifestations. Poor Bonker was a feline binger.

I didn't get the opportunity to treat Bonker, but if I had, environmental enrichment (the get-a-life program) and Prozac would have been high on the agenda, and I would have been optimistic for a good recovery. He would have received more attention, would have been encouraged to play energetic games (particularly of the chase-and-catch variety), and would have found himself surrounded by all sorts of toys to occupy him when his mum was tied up. Cat towers (carpeted rooms with a view) and climbing structures would also have been part of his prescription for good mental and physical health. I would also have advised a more motivated Marsha to get him a compatible roommate, a female perhaps, to satisfy his social needs, and finally I would have discussed dietary restriction. When trying to slim down an overweight cat it is dangerous to attempt to cause the cat to lose weight too rapidly, as liver problems can result. Hepatic lipidosis is the diagnosis you really don't want to hear. Affected cats become jaundiced and often die. If dietary restriction is the way to go, it is best to estimate the weight your cat should be and then feed about 70 percent of the food allowance for a cat of that size to avoid precipitous weight loss. Crash diets are dangerous, especially for cats.

One overweight cat I did have an opportunity to treat came to me by way of my wife's veterinary practice. This twenty-pound, two-and-a-half-year-old neutered male domestic shorthair presented in an unusual but predictable way. For some time my wife had been advising this cat's owners to put the cat on a diet, but her advice fell on stony ground. The months came and went and there were no repercussions for the delinquent owners, but then something happened. One evening they were sitting quietly in their living room when they heard a peculiar faint raspy sound in the background. They looked at each other with surprise. They started to explore around the room and found that the sound got louder in the vicinity of the cat. And then they made the remarkable discovery that it was the cat—breathing. My wife was summoned immediately and gave the cat a thorough physical examination. Other than a mild heart murmur, she found nothing to explain the cat's obvious respiratory difficulty. The cat's lung sounds were clear and all the stridor (noisy breathing) seemed to be emanating from higher up the respiratory tract. The cat's owners were so worried that they requested that the cat be taken to the emergency service at Tufts Veterinary School to see if anything more could be determined by an X ray and other tests. The cat was duly transferred to Tufts, where the doctor on call arranged to have him admitted to the intensive care ward.

The next day my wife, Linda, called up to see what they had found. The answer was nothing in the way of lung disease. The X ray was clear, yet the cat was obviously having difficulty breathing. Their conclusion: the "Pickwickian syndrome" of respiratory failure caused by obesity. That is, the cat was too fat. Author Charles Dickens in his book *The Pickwick Papers* described a character, Mr. Pickwick, who was grossly overweight and had bluish lips. Doctors subsequently recognized that this character suffered from a form of respiratory failure, and the condition has subsequently been described as the Pickwickian syndrome. Obviously Dickens based his characters on real people. Anyway, whatever it is called, this cat had it, and it was caused by being overweight. That's where I came in, although I had listened with interest earlier as the problem unraveled.

Linda and I schemed together on a behavioral and dietary strategy to alleviate this cat's hyperphagic blues. First we suggested getting a kitten to stir things up a bit for the sedentary cat, but the cat's owners weren't too enamored with this idea, having run the gauntlet of additions to the family unsuccessfully before. Infighting had occurred the previous time, and although fighting may be one way for a cat to stay slim, it wasn't exactly what they intended. Our next suggestion was to increase the cat's exercise by spending time with it and encouraging active play. We recommended a cat dancer toy (fishing pole and line) as one tool to assist the owners in this process. I even advised training the cat by the click-and-treat method to encourage positive interactions, but I'm not sure how well that suggestion was received. What the owners seemed most dedicated to was dietary restriction, and they did go ahead and begin giving their cat the same prescription weight-reducing diet I feed my own cats. The results were great. The weight fell off their cat steadily over a period of months. Not too fast, not too slow. Very soon the cat's breathing returned to normal, and we all heaved a sigh of relief.

If overeating is the yin of feline dietary disorders, then under-eating is the yang. Behavior of this type can represent the tip of the iceberg of a condition called separation anxiety. Separation anxiety occurs when a cat is extremely bonded with its owner and then suddenly finds itself alone. The resulting anxiety suppresses the cat's appetite and may result in other symptoms such as inappropriate urination. Each time they are left cats with this condition act as if their owners will not return again and somehow fail to learn that this is not what actually happens. Anorexia occurring during the owners' absence is one of the cardinal signs of separation anxiety. The condition as a whole can be viewed as a transient form of depression, and in many respects this analogy is accurate. Mild forms of the condition respond to behavioral therapy that revolves around desensitization to progressively longer departures of the owner, so that the cat is trained to tolerate being left alone. More-advanced forms of the condition require treatment with antidepressants. Some researchers have drawn parallels between separation anxiety and human panic attacks. This interpretation has some merit. It could be that initial panic following the owner's departure gives way to a state of depression. A depressed mood is sometimes seen in conjunction with separation anxiety in children, although the depression constitutes a separate diagnosis in itself.

The only fortunate thing about separation anxiety (if there can be anything fortunate about such a miserable condition) is that each bout is normally short-lived, lasting only for as long as the owner is away. In other situations, however, including bereavement, the unhappy circumstances prevail, and the misery and associated lack of appetite can be present for months. Here the parallels with human depression are unmistakable. As with humans, the depression may eventually be self-limiting, but some unfortunates continue in a downward spiral until they almost literally fade away to nothing. Treatment with antidepressants is strongly indicated for such cats, as a humane measure if nothing else.

One case of feline depression always haunts me. I was co-consulting with a colleague at our veterinary school when a shabbily dressed woman in her forties arrived in the consulting room clutching her precious bundle, a domestic shorthair cat called Mindy. Eight-year-old Mindy had been doing just fine until her sister and companion, Samantha, passed away after a battle with cancer. The very day that Samantha was taken to the vet's for her final visit Mindy stopped eating, became withdrawn, and slept almost all day every day. Apparently life held no pleasure for her anymore and she seemed determined just to fade into oblivion. This situation had prevailed for some weeks at the time we saw

Mindy. Although the referring vet's instructions to Mindy's owner had been to force-feed her with baby food, Mindy continued to lose weight and was, at the time of her presentation at Tufts, a shadow of her former self. Needless to say, Mindy's owner was extremely upset and willing to try almost anything to get Mindy back on track. I examined Mindy carefully because I knew what sudden fasting could do to a cat, and my worst fears were confirmed. Her mouth and eyes showed the yellow color that is the hallmark of jaundice, and it was apparent that she was in liver failure. A blood sample confirmed hepatic lipidosis, and Mindy was subsequently transferred to the intensive care ward, where she underwent extensive therapy, including intravenous feeding. Mindy was one of the lucky few who survive this type of crisis. She eventually recovered to full health, not least because she received low-dose antidepressant therapy as soon as she was over the immediate biochemical crisis. Mindy's owner eventually acquired another cat as a companion for her and this also must have contributed to her sustained recovery, although I would be willing to bet that Mindy never forgot her sister for as long as she lived—almost like a human. Talk about the hidden life of cats!

More recently I was presented with a slightly less dramatic but nevertheless equally touching case of depression in a seventeen-year-old cat called Stash. Stash's owner didn't know what was wrong with him, not knowing that the label "depressed" could be applied to a cat. She reported two problems. The first was that Stash seemed unhappy and whined a lot, especially at night or early in the morning. The second was that he was not eating regularly and was steadily losing weight. As it turns out, poor Stash had been this way since his brother died eight months earlier. The two cats had been together all their lives and were closely bonded. Then the fateful day arrived when his brother passed away from a kidney complaint, and things were never the same. Stash's owner, Cindy Davis, tried to comfort him, and he would transiently respond to the attention, but he remained far from well. He had lost all interest in play and spent a good deal of the day sleeping. His day was punctuated with occasional tours of the house, presumably to check whether his brother had returned. It was a sad story, but at least there was a happy ending. I treated Stash with Prozac because an antidepressant was indicated and because there wasn't much else I could have done, anyway. It worked. Within a couple of weeks Stash was more like his old self. The whining had stopped, he was happier, and he was eating again. Cindy was delighted with his progress and joined me as a believer in animal depression.

All this talk of panic attacks and depression sounds very much like the human experience, and yet there are differences. A cat, for example, would never get true anorexia nervosa because that requires a degree of self-realization that domestic pets don't appear capable of achieving. Humans with anorexia nervosa believe that they are too fat, whatever their friends, scales, or mirrors tell them. Mirrors are particularly important in sustaining this illusion, and therein lies a tale, because what cats see in mirrors is not themselves but some other cat. Like almost all other species, they react to mirrors with either aggression, fear, or indifference, but not self-interest. Some Old World monkeys may be the only exception to this mirror-mirror-on-the-wall rule, but the subject of animal self-realization remains unclear.

Whatever the motivation for an eating disorder, the bottom line is this: When a cat starts to gain or lose weight, especially if the change occurs suddenly, it's a good idea to pay your local veterinarian a visit to rule out possible medical causes for the condition first. If the result of this visit is a clean bill of health, you should, with your vet's help, try adjusting your cat's diet to correct the discrepancy. This may mean giving less food or a different type of

food to an overweight cat or augmenting the groceries for a slim-
ster. If dietary measures to control the cat's weight are ineffective, it is time to seek expert help in reevaluating the problem, as
it could possibly be a psychogenic disturbance. The circumstances surrounding the start of the eating disorder often throw
valuable light on the conclusion reached. Bear in mind that not
every cat that eats too much has a compulsive eating disorder and
not every cat that undereats is depressed. On the other hand,
appetite is a great indicator of health. Toward the end of a cat's
life, when a veterinarian is evaluating the quality of life remaining
or attempting to determine whether the animal is suffering, the
key question is whether the cat is eating normally. With this in
mind, we should pay careful attention to our cats' eating habits, as
they serve as a barometer for their general and psychological
health and well-being.

Although all this talk about diet and health is valid, it is important to remember that the purpose of life is not simply to live for
eons, for us or for our cats. There are qualitative aspects of life
that also must be considered. Enjoying life is actually more important than winning the respiration marathon, but a compromise
between enjoyment and healthy living seems the most reasonable
solution. In other words, it should be possible to eat one's cake
and have it too; you just can't eat the lot. Good health is an
essential component of a happy life and should be a goal for all of
us to work toward. We should keep this in mind for our pets.
Responsible pet owners should think healthy regarding their
pets' diets and yet be flexible enough to indulge them from time
to time with tidbits of forbidden fruit, as well as attending to
more obvious medical needs.

the run, and have a thing about growing trees in our living rooms. So what's left? Free lunch, a warm place to take a nap afterward, and with luck a window through which to gaze out on life in the real world. Some cats settle into this unnatural existence quite well, particularly if their territory is not invaded and their social life remains stable. They may adapt so well that in time, given the choice between staying in or going out, they will peer nervously at the great outdoors through an open door and then turn around and head in, refusing to cross the threshold. This does not necessarily mean that the environment they live in is optimal. Farm animals that have lived in restricted environments will initially select the familiar prison over the open range, but the selection reverses if the choice is provided frequently enough for them to explore and adjust. For other cats, apartment life is a precarious balance easily disrupted by the comings and goings of other members of the household. The addition of new members to the home, changes in routine, and boredom can take their toll and lead to the kind of behavior problems described in this book.

Some of the fundamental issues cannot be addressed to suit the cat. It's too late for that. We can't stop neutering cats and then let them run around loose on city streets. If we did, we would see worse problems than the ones that we currently see. What we can do, though, is to realize what makes our cats tick, take steps to prevent sudden change, and fill as many of the voids as possible. We can think carefully before adding a new cat to the family and make any such additions gradually. We can provide prey facsimiles and take time to awaken those stalking, hunting, and pouncing instincts. Constructive interactive exercises such as click-and-treat training are also helpful, and good old-fashioned care and affection are musts. In addition, we can provide climbing structures, cat nests, scratching posts, and other environmental enrichment strategies to liven up our cats' surroundings and daily existence. At least we can make the effort, and even if we fall a little short of the ideal, they'll be better off than if we didn't try— and they'll probably understand. After all, we're only human.

Many of the problems that arise in the domestic situation stem from the cat's natural behavioral tendencies. It is often difficult to remember that, size aside, a cat is not far removed from its wild cousins. A cat is in some ways like a miniature tiger in your living room. But despite the obvious differences, we have a lot in common with our wild friends. Territoriality and aggression, dominance and fear, anxiety and compulsions are all very human-sounding drives and emotions. This is hardly surprising when one considers the other side of the coin, our biological relatedness. We both inhabit the third rock from the sun and are warm-blooded mammals more closely related to each other than to a fish or a reptile. We have similar brains with similar control centers and identical chemical messengers. Humans just happen to have a few more corrugations in the cerebral cortex, but who's counting? Our peripheral nervous systems, autonomic nervous systems, and hormonal systems are also so similar that they are discussed in the same breath in physiology class as examples of each other. In light of such striking congruence it is hardly surprising that we experience comparable psychological problems. Cats' response to psychogenic medication alone is a powerful piece of evidence to support the view that cats are sentient creatures with feelings and emotions similar to our own. Why else would an apparently anxious cat have its symptoms alleviated with human anxiety-reducing medication? Although scientists have failed to give full credit to the cat's cognitive abilities because they can't quantify them, the concept of feline intelligence is nothing that would surprise the average cat owner. It will just take time for the pundits to prove what the rest of us already intuitively know to be true: that cats have feelings, too.

ABOUT THE AUTHOR

Nicholas H. Dodman is a veterinarian and director of the Animal Behavior Clinic at Tufts University School of Veterinary Medicine. He graduated from Glasglow University Veterinary School in 1970 and spent some years as a veterinary anesthesiologist before developing his now all-consuming interest in animal behavior. The transition from anesthesiologist to behaviorist was catalyzed by a remarkable discovery he made, along with his colleague Lou Shuster, that some repetitive behaviors in animals are fueled by nature's own morphine-like chemicals, the endorphins. This work led to the first of several U.S. patents that Dr. Dodman holds for ideas regarding behavioral physiology and pharmacology. Dr. Dodman, author of the bestseller *The Dog Who Loved Too Much: Tales, Treatment, and the Psychology of Dogs,* is a nationally recognized leader and innovator in the field of domestic animal behavior. He has published over a hundred scientific articles on subjects ranging from veterinary anesthesiology and pharmacology to animal behavior, and is a board-certified member of the American College of Veterinary Behaviorists.